OLDER AND WISER

Older and Wiser

Classical Buddhist Teachings on
Aging, Sickness, and Death

Mu Soeng
Gloria Taraniya Ambrosia
Andrew Olendzki

BARRE CENTER *for*
BUDDHIST STUDIES

BARRE CENTER FOR BUDDHIST STUDIES

149 Lockwood Road

Barre, MA 01005

bcbs@dharma.org

www.bcbsdharma.org

For ordering copies: please use email or postal address

© Barre Center for Buddhist Studies, 2017

ISBN: 978 1537754574

Cover photo by Elizabeth "Libby" Vidgeon

Contents

Preface   1

Introduction   3

A SHIFT IN FOCUS: A TIME FOR RETIRING

    1.1 Bhaddiya Gets Free   10

    1.2 Ten Things to Reflect Upon   16

    1.3 Higher Pleasures   22

    1.4 Looking Forward to Retirement   28

EQUANIMITY

    2.1 Beyond Joy and Sorrow   34

    2.2 Sleeping Well   40

    2.3 The Single Most Precious Moment   46

    2.4 Two Ways to Prepare   53

AGING

    3.1 The Lucidity of Age   62

    3.2 The Worldly Winds   68

    3.3 The Monk and the King   74

    3.4 Getting Near the End 82

ILLNESS

    4.1 Afflicted in Body—Not in Mind   90

    4.2 Stabbed by One Arrow—Not Two   96

    4.3 Healing Wounds   103

    4.4 Patient and Caregiver   110

DEATH AND DYING

    5.1 The Divine Messengers   118

    5.2 Learning to Let Go   124

    5.3 Taking One's Life   131

    5.4 Facing Death Without Concern   139

6. MOURNING

    6.1 Ānanda Alone   146

    6.2 The Mustard Seed   152

    6.3 Unbearable Grief   159

    6.4 The Soothing of Grief   167

7. PRACTICE

    7.1 The Simile of the Heartwood   174

    7.2 The Parable of Six Creatures   181

    7.3 Working with Fear   187

    7.4 Living in Harmony   193

Suggested Questions for Study Groups   201

    Going Forth: From Home to Homelessness   239

    by Mu Soeng

    Urban Hermit: A Different Way of Being in the World   249

    by Mu Soeng

About the Authors   257

Preface

I suspect that most of you who are reading this book have lived a long time. While we delight in our good fortune, we may also face the very real dilemma of how to use our remaining years in a way that optimizes our prospects for happiness, inner tranquility, and wisdom. Old age has a way of getting our attention, snapping us out of the worldly reverie that can consume us in our youth and well into adulthood. We step into this phase of life with significant natural wisdom—the wisdom that comes with age—and aspire to use our later years to further deepen our understanding of the human condition, our condition. Couple that natural wisdom with the fact that most of us have been (and still are) wholeheartedly drawn to the teachings and practices of the Buddha, and we have a formidable recipe for waking up. All that remains is to be grateful and to apply ourselves to study and contemplation.

This book is offered as a support for that process, to help it along. Originally designed for a program at the Barre Center for Buddhist Studies, we were happy for the chance to adapt it for use by a wider group of readers. We have in the authors a Theravada scholar well-versed in the early teachings of Buddhism, a Zen scholar and practitioner from the Korean Zen tradition, and a lay Buddhist minister and Dhamma teacher rooted in the Thai Forest Tradition—a range of perspectives that, though by no means comprehensive, we hope will speak to diverse interests and points of view. Drawing upon the ancient wisdom of the Buddha as recorded in the early Buddhist scriptures, we offer both scholarly examination and thoughtful reflection on what these teachings mean and how to apply them in our daily life and practice.

Given the depth and breadth of the early Buddhist teachings, there are many other suttas we could have selected. We chose those that align with what we think are the most relevant areas for exploration—retirement (a shift in focus), equanimity, aging, illness, death and dying, mourning, and Dhamma practice.

Each author offers comments and reflections on each sutta. These are limited by our own life experience, understanding at the time of this writing, and simply the spontaneity of the moment. Our hope is that this collection of suttas and essays will stimulate reflection by the reader and spark inquiry beyond these current texts.

To support your study and contemplation, we offer a collection of reflections at the back of the book to accompany each chapter. These can be used both privately by the individual reader and to support study-group discussions, should you wish to organize that in your Dhamma community.

We extend our sincere gratitude to Laura Zimmerman for her priceless advice on how to prepare the text for publication. She is truly a gem and a tireless guide to those of us who lack her skills. We would also like to extend our gratitude to Matt Weingast, Communications Director and Evan Henritze, Online Education Director, both at the Barre Center for Buddhist Studies for their thorough edit and design help.

The Dhamma is a teaching of ageless and timeless wisdom. The verses that we have commented on in this book were uttered over 2500 years ago, and yet they are completely relevant today—especially to those of us going forth into the final chapter of your life. A traditional Buddhist chant asks the question: "The days and nights are relentlessly passing; how well am I spending my time?" Our hope is that, as you contemplate these suttas and our reflections on them, you will enhance your ability to see the relevance of the Dhamma in daily life and to realize the rewards of insight. At this point in our lives you may feel as we do: that such an endeavor represents the best possible use of our time.

~ Gloria Taraniya Ambrosia

Introduction

A Zen story speaks of a young man who appears at the gates of a Zen monastery in Japan and petitions to be admitted into the community. He tells the Zen master that he is a sincere person and is willing to submit himself completely to the discipline but wants some assurance that the practice of Zen will alleviate the one great problem in his life. This problem, he says, is that he is a highly anxious person. The Zen master listens to his story with great sympathy and says that, although highly likely, he cannot guarantee that his specific problem will be resolved through Zen practice.

The young man gets somewhat agitated and asks if Zen practice cannot address this problem of his, what is the point of it? The Zen master explains that regardless of whether or not his anxiety problem can be resolved, the one outcome that can be guaranteed in Zen practice is that "it will allow you to meet the moment of your death with courage and dignity."

This story may seem quite strange to our modern ears and sensibilities, and may even appear as one of those crazy Zen stories that don't really speak to the question. But it also has the possibility of setting up several intriguing nuances. The first of these is the conventional view of what is politely called "later years," which is often contrasted with a cheerful indulgence in "youth."

We have been conditioned in our contemporary Western culture to view our later years as a time of decline and diminishing capabilities, which usually inculcates a defeatist attitude. By contrast, we are conditioned to celebrate the youth culture and all the hedonistic pleasures associated with it. In our story, the young man is asked to spend the rest of his life in contemplation of death and dying. This is counterintuitive and goes against our cultural conditioning.

By contrast, in traditional Asian societies, the journey between earlier and later years is often marked by the pursuit of wisdom. In this reckoning, wisdom can be pursued by younger people with as much diligence as it is attended to by older people.

Another nuance in our story is the cultivation of awareness of death as a holistic approach to life itself. Zen tradition uses the phrase "this great matter of life and death" to speak of the inseparability of life and death. An authentic understanding of our life/existence cannot be truly fruitful unless it incorporates a sensibility of transience and insubstantiality of the phenomenal world—its decay and dissolution—including our own bodies.

Physicists tell us that our universe is governed by the laws of entropy—both the expansion and the compression of matter. The universe out there is being created and destroyed in each microsecond. As soon as things are created, there's an inherent tension between their existence and upcoming dissolution. We rearrange cosmic matter and energy into our own body with its complex chemistry and neural pathways. It took four billion years of self-engineering for an encoded system to emerge that is functionally self-enclosed and subject to the tension of creation and dissolution at the subatomic level. As an infinitesimal part of the universe, the system of our bodies is also governed by the laws of entropy.

The cultivation of wisdom helps us to understand, investigate, and internalize this tension between existence and disintegration, and thus engender a sense of fearlessness— "dignity and courage" as spoken of in our Zen story. This sense of fearlessness is what helps us negotiate the great matter of life and death, both in our younger and in our later years. Is this not the most important task for us as human beings—to remain equanimous even while looking the terror of death in the face?

We encounter this terror whenever we have to face the unknown and the uncertain. The cultivation of wisdom, whether we are young or old, is to relate to this terror with fearlessness. The teachings of the Buddha tell us that the cultivation of wisdom and fearlessness is engendered through letting go—through non-clinging. It is in letting go of all our conceptions and constructions about life and death that we truly engage with "this great matter of life and death."

The famous last words uttered by the Buddha have come down to us as: "All compounded phenomena are subject to decay. Strive on diligently." (Pāli: *Vāyadhamma sankhāra. Appamādena sampadetha.*)

The Pali word *appamādena* literally means "through heedfulness" which can also be understood as being fearless. The translation of the word as "striving on diligently" is used here in a broader sense as an embodiment of fearlessness in our psychological and emotional structures whether we are young, middle-aged, or older.

The Buddha himself was working within the contexts of certain arrangements of society in which the so-called retirement years were seen as a time for the eventual fulfillment of one's life. These arrangements called for four distinct phases of one's life: 1) as a "student," where one is expected to remain celibate, learn a trade or profession, train in martial arts if one belongs to a warrior class, or train in conducting rites and rituals if one belongs to a priestly class; 2) as a householder, fully participating in a family life—copulation, reproduction, civic and familial duties, and so on; 3) as a "retiree," where husband and wife together leave all familial responsibilities and join other spiritual strivers in a community in the forest; 4) the last stage of life where one leaves even the community behind and walks on into the mountains to be alone and look into the face of death with the courage and dignity one has cultivated in the third phase of life. (This arrangement of society is discussed at length in the essay at the end of this book, *Going Forth as Psychological Homelessness.*)

While this arrangement of society and its concomitant value system may seem puzzling and counterintuitive to our contemporary ways of thinking, there seems to be an inherent creativity in this vision of one's elder years. The third stage of life is not necessarily marked with social or psychological isolation. A necessary ingredient for this stage of life, however, is the giving up of striving for hedonistic comfort that may have been the hallmark of a householder's life, the second stage of life.

In this arrangement, it is understood that one's existence is more a matter of performing one's "duty" (another translation of the word "dharma") rather than living a life of indolence and indulgence. It is also understood that the cultivation of wisdom starts early with an internalization of the four stages of life and the duties, responsibilities, and values associated with each stage.

In this context, growing older also means growing into wisdom. The wisdom most associated with aging, sickness, and dying is to see it as a natural and organic process—not alien to life, but rather as the very nature of life itself: what comes to be ceases to be. Whatever comes to be has only a momentary and transient existence.

Among the many similes used by the Buddha, the following is a terse reminder of the transience of life:

Form is like a glob of foam;
feeling, a bubble;
perception, a mirage;
fabrications, a banana tree;
consciousness, a magic trick —
    this has been taught
    by the Kinsman of the Sun.
However you observe them,
appropriately examine them,
they're empty, void
    to whoever sees them
    appropriately.   *(Samyutta Nikaya 22:95)*

These sentiments have been echoed, perhaps even more poetically, in the famous Diamond Sutra (the *Vajracheddika Prajnaparamita Sutra*) as follows:

> So you should see [view] all of the fleeting world:
> a star at dawn, a bubble in the stream;
> a flash of lightning in a summer cloud;
> a flickering lamp, phantom and a dream.

The wisdom teachings of the Buddha caution us that our engagement with the issues of sickness, aging, and dying will be truly fruitful only when a perceptual-cognitive shift as suggested in the above passages takes place. This shift can come about only through the long and consistent practice of mindfulness, which leads to fearlessness, which leads to equanimity.

Contemporary Western practitioners are no longer in the world of the young man knocking on the doors of the Zen monastery, but the matter of life and death persists for us just as intensely. The issues of aging, sickness, and dying have been difficult for every human being who has ever lived, and each one of us has to learn how to deal with these issues. The teachings of the Buddha offer a unique approach to engaging with these issues, and this engagement is the subject of essays in this volume.

The reflections in this volume were originally addressed to a self-selected group of Buddhist practitioners embarking on their retirement years and/or dealing with issues of aging, sickness, and dying for themselves or for their loved ones. The engagement with these issues was framed through how Buddhist practices and Buddhist teachings deal with the "great matter of life and death."

The selected passages from the Pāli Canon and reflections on them are offered here to a wider audience in the understanding that it is never easy to die. Nor is it ever easy to live. As human beings, we look to various sources—religious, social, economic, political—to help us navigate matters of life and death. The reflections here suggest looking to our inner wisdom as a primary source.

May all humans live wisely and die joyfully.

~Mu Soeng

1. A Shift In Focus: A Time For Retiring

10 • Older and Wiser

1.1 Bhaddiya Gets Free

Bhaddiya was a great Sakya chieftain, the son of the matriarch Kāli-Godhā whom the Buddha identifies as the most high-born person in his circle. He is very likely the one who stepped into the position of Sakya leadership left vacant when Siddhartha left home to become a wanderer. He was good friends with Anuruddha, the Buddha's cousin (and Ānanda's brother), who persuaded him to go forth with him into the homeless life under the Buddha's instruction. Both friends, like Siddhartha, enjoyed a privileged upbringing and had to make some adjustments to the renunciate life of a wandering bhikkhu.

At one point Bhaddiya was overheard uttering the phrase, "Ah, what bliss! Ah, what bliss!" while sitting alone in the wilderness, and his fellow monks suspected that he was remembering the pleasures of his earlier life and thus not engaging fully in the rigors of forest practice. When called before the Buddha to account for himself, it turns out that just the opposite was true. He is reported in the Vinaya to have explained the matter to the Buddha in the following way:

"Formerly, when I was a ruler, there was a fully appointed guard both within my private quarters and outside … both within the town and outside … and throughout the countryside. But although being guarded and warded thus, I dwelt afraid, anxious, fearful, and alarmed. But now, dwelling in a forest and at the root of a tree and in an empty place, I am unafraid, not anxious, not fearful and not alarmed. I am unconcerned, unruffled, dependent on others, with a mind become as a wild creature's. This is why I was uttering the phrase, 'Ah, what bliss! Ah, what bliss!'" (*Cullavagga 7:1.6*)

Twenty-six stanzas of verse attributed to Bhaddiya are preserved in the *Theragāthā*, the poems of the elder monks, including these:

Soft were the clothes worn by me then,
Riding on an elephant's neck,
Eating only the finest rice,
With delectable meat sauces.

Today, fortunate and happy,
Pleased by any scraps in his bowl,
Bhaddiya, the son of Godhā,
Meditates without any grasping.

With lofty, encircling walls,
Firm battlements and sturdy gates,
Guarded by many, sword in hand,
I dwelt in the city—frightened!

Today, fortunate, unafraid,
Devoid of any fear or dread,
Bhaddiya, the son of Godhā,
Meditates while plunged in the woods.

Established in integrity,
Developing mindfulness and
Wisdom, I attained, step by step,
The dissolution of all bonds.

(Theragāthā 842-865)

Reflections: Andrew Olendzki

There can be no doubt that many benefits ensue from a position of power and privilege. Less well acknowledged is the price one must often pay to sustain these. In Bhaddiya's case he seemed to have some concern about being assassinated; for those in the modern world who shoulder significant responsibilities, there might be heavy pressures to produce results, anxiety about the many things that might go wrong, a secret insecurity that one might not really have what it takes to succeed, or simply the relentlessness of having each morning to roll the boulder up the hill one more time.

Bhaddiya's companions in the life of practice assumed the mainstream interpretation that having it all is wonderful and that practicing in the forest with nothing involves a great diminution. He must thus be lost in reverie, they think, reliving the "good old days." Just the opposite turns out to be true, of course. Bhaddiya has discovered the counterintuitive insight that he is much happier when relieved of the burdens of his former position. With nothing to lose, there is nothing to protect. Having nothing to protect brings peace of mind and a higher form of well-being: "Ah, what bliss!" I suspect prince Siddhartha discovered a similar sense of relief and freedom when he wandered forth into the "wide open spaces" of the homeless life.

Might not settling into one's elder phase of life yield a similar insight? Yes, it is gratifying to have an important job, perhaps earn a lot of money, have co-workers and family members depend upon you, or provide a crucial service for those you care about. These responsibilities have also been known, however, to be accompanied by considerable mental and physical stress, to raise the blood pressure to unhealthy levels, to force the mind to do so many things at once that none of them can be done very well, and generally to contribute to an experience of feeling trapped. The walls that protect us also imprison us.

The bonds that are slipped by Bhaddiya are both tangible and intangible. Buddha teaches the release of the mind from such mental fetters as sense desire, ill will, conceit, ignorance, and doubt, and this profound psychological transformation is facilitated by a lifestyle released from the constraints of worldly duties and responsibilities. In ancient India the free lifestyle was that of a wandering ascetic. Perhaps today a similar lifestyle can be carved out by a person whose children are grown and settled, whose professional career has tapered off or concluded, and who finally has the time to focus attention more fully upon understanding the enduring challenges of the human condition.

The various bonds constraining the mind, some socially imposed, others more uniquely personal, have been forged over a lifetime of conditioning. It requires time, energy, and commitment to learn to see, understand, and gradually free the mind from their grip. But what nobler thing can there be to do with what remains of this precious human birth?

Reflections: Mu Soeng

In line with the Buddha's frequent use of metaphors in speaking to his audiences, this particular passage is chock-full of metaphors. It may be possible to see the "city" here as the self that is constructed by each one of us in our own unique way. Although the details of the construction of both the "self" and the "city" may differ greatly, there is a certain universality in its "fortifications." These fortifications around an individual self are various filters of "I, me, mine" that are put into place to assess and assimilate (or disassociate from) each encounter with internal or external phenomena, with gatekeepers who decide which visitors to admit and which to turn away.

Yet within these seemingly reassuring fortifications there is a constant fear among the rulers that they can be breached. Reasonable or irrational as that fear may be, the constructed self also finds itself threatened by the thought of death. However, as the Buddhist thinker David Loy has pointed out, "from the Buddhist perspective our primary repression is not of death-terror but another fear even more fundamental: the suspicion that 'I' am not real. Rather than being autonomous in some Cartesian fashion, our sense of self is mentally and social conditioned, therefore ungrounded and (as the mentally ill remind us) fragile."

Each individual's intuition that the "city" of "I" is ultimately indefensible due to its constantly shifting nature is one of the deepest yet un-recovered insights for human beings. Our foolish human conditioning wants to continue to imagine this "I" as being defensible, and therefore gathers all sorts of possessions within its fortified wings. It is only by claiming ownership of these possessions that the conditioned/constructed self can feel secure.

The counter-metaphor of the forest being the safest place, despite it being unguarded and without fortification, is the core teaching of the Buddha: embracing the essential *lack* in the constructed self. The term "lack" is David Loy's creative reinterpretation of the Pāli term *anattā*, and it speaks eloquently to the realization that it is only the constructed self that needs to be fortified and defended. The embracing of self-as-lack is, like the forest, the metaphorical space where integrity and mindfulness develop and where, step-by-step, wisdom is attained.

The "dissolution of all bonds" may be seen as yet another metaphor for letting go of all possibility of owning anything in this radically impermanent phenomenal world. Letting go allows us to rethink our engagements with the inevitable processes of sickness, aging, and dying. On one hand this rethinking, grounded in our disciplined meditation practice and insight, has the effect of calming the deleterious impact of whatever mental pathology there might be in dealing with these biological processes. On the other hand, letting go of all imagined possibilities of ownership, as taught by the Buddha, is how to not only remain blissful in the diligence of mindfulness, but also to become free of the flotsam of the "floating world."

Reflections: Gloria Taraniya Ambrosia

Each year I visit one or more of the forest monasteries in the lineage of Ajahn Chah and stay for at least a few weeks, if not a few months. Life for the laity in these monasteries involves taking up the discipline of monastic life and directly supporting the nuns and monks. I deliberately place myself in this renunciate world so that I can experience life in a simpler way—unburdened with obligations and responsibilities, roles, and identities. Monastic life is not without its duties and routines. We get up at 4am for morning meditation and chanting, and our days are filled with chores around the residences, help in the kitchen, work on the buildings and grounds, and meditation. But over time the simplicity of monastic life does help to quiet the mind. One isn't distracted by the things of the world—fancy objects, food, entertainment, or social events. One begins to see the value of putting all of this aside, at least temporarily, and devoting oneself to contemplation. For me, doing so is enormously helpful, even blissful!

I began this annual trek nearly thirty years ago, and now that I am clearly entering my so-called golden years, I see the parallels between lay versus monastic life and youth versus old age. As we move into the final chapters of our lives, many of us are downsizing, simplifying, and letting go of the complexities of Western culture that complicate our lives. Rather than accumulating more ... many of us are asking how to live with less. Like Bhaddiya, we seek to move beyond worldly aims and values to experience the bliss associated with doing and having less. I'll never forget a retreatant in the closing circle of her first three-month retreat joyfully exclaiming, "I didn't know I could live with so little."

I don't want to overstate the importance of living with less. Some of us may not choose to downsize, and that is fine. (For myself, I have found it necessary to keep my worldly attachments to a minimum—not because I think I should or because it is the right way to be, but because I am so easily distracted by them!) But even if we are not actively trying to live with less ... I suspect we can all relate to an increasing attraction to letting go internally. Perhaps we have seen and felt the pain of attachment enough to begin to find our ground outside of it.

One could easily see the story of Bhaddiya as pointing to the greater inherent joy of monastic life. Interpreted in this narrow way, it may not speak to those of us who have chosen to live the life of a householder. It may even seem to challenge that choice. Thus, we might turn away from this teaching, thinking it doesn't apply to us.

However, a broader interpretation offers much for those of us who seek to move beyond entanglement in the world. Our "golden" years could well be the very best years of our lives if we know what to do with them ... and dare to do it. With right reflection, there is the real potential for enjoying the bliss of non-attachment and exiting this world with smiles on our faces.

16 • Older and Wiser

1.2 Ten Things to Reflect Upon

There are these ten things that one who has gone forth should often reflect upon.

One who has gone forth should often reflect:

1. I have entered upon a classless condition.

2. My living is dependent upon others.

3. My behavior should be different.

4. Do I reproach myself in regard to virtuous behavior?

5. Do my wise companions, having investigated, reproach me in regard to virtuous behavior?

6. I must be parted and separated from everyone and everything dear and agreeable to me.

7. I am the owner of my action, the heir of my action; I have action as my origin, action as my relative, action as my resort; I will be the heir of whatever action, good or bad, that I do.

8. How am I spending my nights and days?

9. Do I take delight in empty huts?

10. Have I attained any distinction in knowledge and vision worthy of the noble ones, so that in my last days, when I am questioned by my companions, I will not be embarrassed?

(Anguttara Nikāya 10:48)

Reflections: Andrew Olendzki

These ten questions are directed by the Buddha to monks and nuns who have gone forth into the homeless state of the wandering monastic in ancient India. The same questions can be fruitfully reinterpreted and reflected upon in ways that pertain to those who have gone forth into the retirement phase of life in modern times.

We invite each of you to do this in your own way, but here are a few suggestions.

The 'retiree' might be thought of as a class in itself, similar to the class of 'monastic,' both being defined by what they are not. A retired person may not be actively practicing a profession, may not be currently raising children, may not be marching with the army—one has retired from such things.

Everyone lives in dependence with everyone else on one level, yet there is a significant shift when one no longer earns a salary and lives on a fixed income, whether based on savings or pensions and social security. By disengaging from active participation in economic affairs, one may gain a heightened sensitivity to the interdependence of all its components.

The next three questions have to do with living a life of ethical integrity. We are used to thinking of reproach as a judgment or condemnation, but in Buddhist circles it is considered a generous act one companion on the path can offer to another. Absent a sensitive personal ego, one would welcome feedback and correction to one's behavior as the powerful ally it can be to living impeccably.

The sixth question goes right to the bone. It is a continual reminder of impermanence, of the passing away of all phenomena. This inevitably involves the loss of what is held dear, but also encompasses all that is distressing or painful—this too shall pass.

The word for action here is, of course, kamma (karma). Each moment we inherit a personality from a lifetime of previous habit-formation, and this influences how meaning gets constructed anew individually. And each moment we also have an opportunity to revise that inheritance, modifying who we will become in the future by how we respond to things in the present.

The eighth question pierces even the bone and gets to the marrow of things. As one Pāli poem puts it, "*Days and nights go rushing by, as your life hurtles to its end.*" (*accayanti ahorattā, jīvitam uparujjhati.*) In Buddhist contexts this is not a morbid or fearful thought, but rather an invitation to wake up, pay attention, and participate in what is happening while you have the privilege of doing so.

Monks and nuns meditated in empty huts, but this is also a general metaphor for silent practice. Does one look forward to sitting and delight in the tranquility and clarity? At this stage of life, meditation should not be a chore, but a blessing.

The final reflection reminds us that the ultimate benefit of a life well led and a mind well developed is wisdom. Understanding the nature of things here on this earth and here in our lives and here, this moment, in our bodies and minds, is a noble end in itself. In the ending moments of our lives, it can be a source of great dignity to feel that one has understood what is to be understood and seen things as they actually are.

Reflections: Mu Soeng

These ten guidelines for someone who has "gone forth" speak to a fundamental paradigm of self-sufficiency. Although there is no precise word in Pali for self-sufficiency, the term *sampuṇṇa* (literally, being full or complete) captures a faint sense of living a life in which self-reliance and self-responsibility may be conjoined with self-sufficiency to create a holistic gestalt.

This gestalt may be reimagined in our own contemporary thinking as not depending on anyone else or anything external for one's own sense of well-being. Our own "going forth" into retirement years—into aging processes, into oncoming death— has parallels with someone going forth from a householder's life to a homeless life in the Buddha's community. Both embark upon new "training steps" (*sikkhāpadaṁ*) to embrace a new phase in one's life for which there are plenty of lessons to be learned from those who have gone before us.

In the Buddhist community of wandering monks, there are well-established protocols for how to hold oneself and carry oneself forward in the world (the "world" being interactions with people who support the monks through donations of food, clothing, and shelter, as well as the world of the unexpected while moving through glens and forests).

This moving through glens and forests and encountering the unexpected and the unknown may be a metaphor for our own encounter with our "declining" years. We have ideas about how we would like to make optimal use of these years, but we need to prepare ourselves for unexpected difficulties due to unplanned infirmities, which might put a limit on what we can and cannot do.

If we adopt the ten things mentioned in this text as a way to prepare for all eventualities, our passage through our elder years could be much more harmonious. The broad theme here seems to be a series of relinquishments and realignments in our emotional and psychological lives, which are going to be forced upon us in our elder years whether we are prepared for them or not. So, why not prepare for them now?

Take, for example, reflection #3. Our deportment has to be different at every stage of life, and our maturing process involves being comfortable with changing our deportment as the situation demands. So, if you are in your seventies and you have a heart condition, you might need to accept with equanimity the fact that you might not be able to run a marathon, even though your neighbor in the same age group is able to do that. You don't need to feel envious of the neighbor.

Or take reflection #6—that we must be parted from all that's dear and agreeable to us. As we get older, we don't have the same emotional energy to invest in things that were formerly dear and agreeable. To accept this lack of emotional energy as a natural part of our elder years is to give ourselves the gift of harmony with things as they are.

I like to think that each of us can adopt these ten reflections, much as we can adopt the many verses of the Dhammapada as metaphors and similes, for living our life in a wholesome gestalt. Every time I read the verses of the Dhammapada they speak in a new and different way, even when I read the same verse after a gap of some time. In the same way, these ten reflections are timeless.

Reflections: Gloria Taraniya Ambrosia

The Buddha offered this sutta to the ordained community. It reflects a high standard of renunciation—higher, perhaps, than we as lay people may be living. But as we age and drop some of the worldly values and trappings of our younger years, the standards kept by householders begin to blend or merge with those of the monastic community. Thus, we can turn to this sutta and find useful reflections.

I'd like to home in on the fourth recollection—"Do I reproach myself in regard to virtuous behavior?" This has to do with remorse for our conduct.

It is quite natural as we grow older to take stock of our lives. In the process, we often uncover feelings of remorse or regret for things we have said or left unsaid, for things we have done or left undone. These tend to reverberate in the mind as unfinished business. Generally speaking, this internal evaluation can be quite useful. But before putting too much energy into it, we would be wise to make sure we understand the distinction between remorse and regret. These are not synonymous. Remorse is highly valued in the Buddhist teachings; regret is not. Remorse is a valued quality because it causes us to open our hearts to the way we are, to the way we have been, to our so-called sins of commission and omission. We stop turning away from our conduct or explaining it away. Instead, we get real about our actions through body, speech, and mind. We stay with the feeling of harm, so to speak, and open to it. This is how we protect ourselves from repeating harmful actions; in a paradoxical way, it helps us find peace.

Regret, on the other hand, manifests as anxiety or restless agitation in the mind. The mind goes over and over what we have done and cannot let it go. It is as if the mind is trying to fix the harm or make it go away. You may recognize this agitation as *uddhacca-kukkucca*, the mental hindrance of restlessness and worry. It serves no useful purpose.

The Buddha spoke about two natural factors that are organically active in a mind that is free from confusion and fear. *Hiri* is the remorse or shame we feel at prospects of doing harm … or even the memory of having done so. And *ottappa* is a kind of self-respect that causes us to shrink from doing harm again. These two work together. When *hiri* is well developed, the heart aches with the feeling of remorse. When we allow ourselves to fully feel remorse without ill-will or judging, we cultivate *ottappa*, the ability to withdraw from the impulse to do harm in the future. *Hiri* and *ottappa* are uplifted states of mind. Together, these support the ability to differentiate between what is worthy of respect and what is not. They are called the guardians of the universe, and one can see why. If we have a healthy dose of *hiri* and *ottappa*, we are truly worthy of respect and can walk this earth in harmlessness. (See also *7.3: Working with Fear*)

As we review our lives and remember certain times when we behaved in less than skillful or optimal ways, let's open our hearts to that reality. If there is remorse … that's a good thing. "Do I reproach myself in regard to virtuous behavior?" If the answer is "yes," we are in good shape. Living without regret does not mean living without remorse. We need to understand this, see the distinction between the two, and open to the highly valued feeling of remorse.

1.3 Higher Pleasures

Formerly, when I lived the home life, I enjoyed myself,
provided and endowed with the five cords of sensual pleasure:
- with forms cognizable by the eye ...
- with sounds cognizable by the ear ...
- with odors cognizable by the nose ...
- with flavors cognizable by the tongue ...
- with tangibles cognizable by the body

that are wished for, desired, agreeable, and likeable,
connected with sensual desire and provocative of lust.

I had three palaces, one for the rainy season,
one for the winter, and one for the summer.
I lived in the rains' palace for the four months of the rainy season,
enjoying myself with musicians, none of whom were men,
and I did not go down to the lower palace.

On a later occasion,
having understood as they actually are
- the origin,
- the disappearance,
- the gratification,
- the danger, and
- the escape

in the case of sensual pleasures,
I abandoned craving for sensual pleasures,
I removed fever for sensual pleasures,
and I abide without thirst, with a mind inwardly at peace.

I see other beings who are not free from lust for sensual pleasures
being devoured by craving for sensual pleasures,
burning with fever for sensual pleasures,
indulging in sensual pleasures,
and I do not envy them, nor do I delight therein.

Why is that? Because there is a delight apart from sensual pleasures, apart from unwholesome states, which surpasses even divine bliss. Since I take delight in that,
I do not envy what is inferior,
nor do I delight therein.

(Māgandiya Sutta, Majjhima Nikāya 75)

Reflections: Andrew Olendzki

This is one of the autobiographical passages of the Pāli Canon in which the Buddha, speaking from his own experience, describes both the benefits and drawbacks of his life in the palace before leaving to embark on his spiritual path. As gratifying as the sensual pleasures of such a lifestyle were, the craving, fever, and thirst for them can be seen as a great affliction. I think he gained this perspective only after he left home and experienced a different kind of pleasure, one not dependent on sensual gratification but which arises when the pursuit of pleasure is abandoned altogether. It turns out that freedom *from* pleasure, so to speak, is a higher pleasure than the pleasures of the senses. Being healed of the fever of being caught up with pleasure, his mind was able to experience an inner peacefulness.

The Buddha here contrasts the view of things one has before and after going forth. What he says about going forth into the homeless life of the wandering ascetic might just as well be said of one who has gone forth into retirement. Those rich in years can probably look back at times in their lives when they were successful in one way or another, something that can of course be measured in many different ways. Perhaps it was a period of financial ascendance, a time of happy family life, or perhaps there was some professional accomplishment, social recognition, or a particularly meaningful friendship. One can appreciate the gratification of such times—it feels good and brings with it many benefits. Such memories may be among our most precious possessions.

It is customary to mourn the loss of good things that have happened to us in the past, and to presume that if we are in comparatively diminished circumstances later, we must be worse

24 • Older and Wiser

off. As we look back on such things with perspective, however, we may be able to recognize certain benefits associated with no longer being in the midst of such times. While something is lost, something else of great value may also be gained. The conventional wisdom is that having it all is what it is all about. And when one is caught up in the midst of acquiring, maintaining, and protecting one's accomplishments, it can indeed feel like a sort of relentless fever. But from a more mellow and sober perspective—one that can come with age and retirement from the struggle—one might acquire an appreciation of the pleasures of serenity that could not be accessed while in the swirl of the fray.

The pleasure of not having and not needing to have is subtler than that of sensual gratification, but the Buddha's point is not only that it is not a lesser pleasure, but that it is a far greater pleasure. He has no envy for those still in the midst of things who are "devoured by craving" and "burning with fever." He enjoys instead "a mind inwardly at peace." This was—and is—one of the many blessings of having "gone forth."

Reflections: Mu Soeng

It has often been pointed out that the Buddha's antidote to the problem of *dukkha* (suffering; stress; anguish; unsatisfactoriness) is non-clinging. This autobiographical passage from the Buddha speaks literally as well as metaphorically to the notion of "going forth" as a movement from craving and clinging to non-craving and non-clinging. The Buddha was a systems-thinker, much along the line of today's research scientists. Thus, when he points to the layered construction of craving he sees it as a "system" that has 1) the origin, 2) the disappearance, 3) the gratification, 4) the danger, and 5) the escape (of and from sensual pleasures).

We learn from current research in neurochemistry that sensual pleasures create a "reward system" in the neural pathways of the brain; they become addictions in a literal sense. The range of such addiction might stretch from the merely psychological and the emotional to a kind of drug experience. As Robert Wright, the evolutionary psychologist, has said, "Habituation to any goal—

sex or power, say—is literally an addictive process, a growing dependence on the biological chemicals that make these things gratifying."

For the Buddha, the urge for gratification through sensual desires is not different from the drug addictions we are familiar with, and he considers them a "lower pleasure." His exhortation to see the danger as well as the need to escape from the lower pleasure is the same caution that a medical doctor would offer against drug addiction. The intoxication of sex and power (not to speak of fame and wealth), among other addictions, is an ever-escalating process in which gratification becomes a self-enclosed goal and purpose of existence without a satisfying happiness coming out of it. The Buddha called this intoxication "thirst" or *taṇhā,* which then becomes a "fever." The fever/thirst/craving, in Buddha's estimation, is a "burning" that can burn away one's ability to think and act in wholesome and beneficial ways.

By contrast, the "higher pleasure" comes from cooling off (one phrase for *nibbāna* is *sīti-bhūta,* which means "cooling") the burning and the feverishness that come from pursuit of gratification of sensual pleasures. The Buddha says there is a "delight apart from sensual pleasures" and that he abides "without thirst, with a mind inwardly at peace."

We all have had the experience at one point or another in our formal meditation practice when we are completely at rest and the mind is inwardly at peace, without any movement toward a desired object/thought or away from an undesirable object/thought. This lack of movement is a lack of thirst in a very physiologically identifiable sense, and the lack of thirst is its own reward, for it brings a peace of mind that cannot be adequately categorized. Here, lack has been turned upside-down to function as fulfillment without craving for sensual pleasure.

This turning of lack into fulfillment was a revolution brought about by the Buddha in his approach to human existence and its discontents. The habituated way to exist is to seek gratification in sensual pleasures without being aware of the likelihood that such pursuit might give rise to addictive patterns in the brain. The insights into the nature of craving itself—seeing its origin, seeing its dependent nature, seeing its momentary existence, seeing its danger, and choosing not to act upon it—amount to what we might today call an evolutionary psychology, in the sense of being evolved. If followed as a path, this evolved or evolutionary psychology translates into higher pleasure.

We can translate all of this into how we deal with the processes of aging and, eventually, dying. We can translate what we see as a lack in these processes into a fulfillment that comes from resting in non-clinging to anything at all in this very moment.

Reflections: Gloria Taraniya Ambrosia

Much of our youth is spent seeking, enjoying … even indulging in sensual pleasures. Our definitions of happiness revolve around worldly accomplishments and delights, and so we seek and enjoy gratification at that level. And it makes perfect sense. We are operating out of a worldly understanding of happiness and, as such, worldly delights fit the bill. But as we age we begin to notice how … for all our effort … we never seem to settle into a state of lasting satisfaction.

This sutta outlines the conditions whereby we realize imperturbable peace of mind … a peace that rests outside the realm of worldly delights. It's a teaching that we see echoed throughout the Buddhist teachings. The Buddha says that by seeing sense pleasures as they actually are—seeing their origin, disappearance, gratification, danger, and escape—he went beyond superficial happiness and arrived at profound peace of mind. In other words, by contemplating sense pleasures in terms of these five points and letting the commensurate insights take hold, he awakened to a deeper experience of happiness.

It is for us to discover for ourselves what this process is all about. Our task as practitioners is to walk through these same five realizations. But it's not as if we have to go about this process in a formulaic way. The truth is … if we have been attentive through the years … these insights are already beginning to sink in.

Through the years we notice that sensory pleasure is *arising* of its own accord—that is, it is arising out of conditions. The experience of pleasure is impersonal. Yes, WE feel it ... and that is why it is experienced as personal. But its arising is outside of our control. You only have to plan family gatherings over the holidays, for example, to realize that this is true. No matter how much we set it up so that everyone will have a great time, something easily (and inevitably!) goes in another direction. Pleasure arises out of conditions over which we have no control.

Over time we also see the *disappearance* of sense pleasures— that is, while we follow craving with its promise of easy happiness, sooner or later we notice that we never feel gratified once and for all. No matter how great the pleasure, it is always impermanent.

We see the *gratification* of sense pleasures. It is interesting that the Buddha doesn't deny the pleasures of the sensory world— neither here nor elsewhere. In this excerpt from the *Māgandiya Sutta*, he describes in some detail the undeniable pleasure of his worldly life, then leaps to when he saw through the lure of worldly pleasure and enjoyed an even greater happiness—a delight that exists apart from sense pleasures. As we, too, realize this, we see the *danger*, drawbacks, or disadvantages of sense pleasures. They pale by comparison to the end of craving ... the unworldly pleasure of renunciation or letting go. At last, we realize the *escape*. We abide without thirst and enjoy inner peace.

Ajahn Chah called *nibbāna* "the reality of non-grasping." Even with only a moment's escape, an inkling into the truth of this teaching, our lives can be changed dramatically.

28 • Older and Wiser

1.4 Looking Forward to Retirement

When indeed shall I dwell in a mountain cave,
Utterly alone and without companion,
Seeing the impermanence of all existence?
This, for me—When shall it at last come to be?

When indeed shall I bear the sage's torn robe,
Yellow-clad, unselfish, and without a fault,
With greed, hatred, and delusion vanquished,
Dwelling happily, having gone to the woods?

When shall I see this impermanent body
With insight, as a hoary nest of disease,
Besieged by aging and death, and dwell fearless
Alone in the woods? When shall it come to be?

When shall I dwell, taking hold of the sharpened sword
Made of wisdom to cut through the vine of craving
That twines so insidiously, giving birth to fear
And conveying such pain—When shall this come to be?

When the deva has rained, the grass is four-fingers tall,
And the forest is a shimmering cloud of blossoms,
I will sit on a stump in the heart of the hills
—And to me that will be as soft as cotton.

(Theragāthā 1190-1195)

Reflections: Andrew Olendzki

Tālaputa, the author of these verses, was the head of a troupe of actors in Rājagaha, the capital city of Magadha in the time of the Buddha. His company travelled all over India and was quite famous; perhaps he was the ancient world's equivalent of a celebrity. This is only an extract from a much longer poem, and the eloquent, theatrical, almost melodramatic style we glimpse here is carried throughout. It has the flavor of an urbane city-dweller who is looking forward with great longing to his retirement by going forth as a Buddhist monk. He yearns for the simple life of a mendicant, living alone in the forest and practicing the path to awakening. Though he seems willing to take on the hardships of life in the wilderness, he may be suspected of idealizing it somewhat as well.

One cannot help respecting and honoring his intention. In the first stanza he yearns for solitude. One can imagine a life lived largely in company, at parties and public functions, in the homes of the wealthy and the courts of the powerful. Not unlike Bhaddiya, the Sakyan chieftain who revels in the joy of solitude (See 1.1: *Bhaddiya Gets Free*), or like Siddhartha himself, the actor imagines the pleasures of a quieter life.

In the second stanza we find a penchant for simplicity and humility, the life of a monk in the forest who has few desires. Indeed, desire is the very thing that complicates any life, as one wish after another rises up to demand satisfaction and we hustle endlessly to assuage them all. Only when greed and hatred, the root causes of preferring one thing over another, are finally put to rest can one obtain peace of mind.

The third stanza has to do with the ability to look upon one's body as impermanent and subject to aging, illness, and death—and yet to do so without fear. This requires insight and the deep wisdom to know the nature of things. Well-being comes from placing oneself in harmony with the way things are rather than trying to fight against nature, an understanding that comes with age and maturity.

In the fourth stanza we encounter an image common to the Mahayana tradition but rare in the early texts, that of wisdom as a sword. The emphasis in the later tradition is on cutting through delusion, while here we see the sword slicing through craving, depicted as a creeping vine that must be severed to bring an end to both fear and pain. (It is interesting that fear comes up twice, in adjacent verses.)

The last section of this extract focuses on the lovely image of sitting in meditation amid the bounties of nature. He specifies that this is after the rainy season, when the forest is exploding with new growth and the trees and bushes are blooming. Tālaputa is setting a scene of an imagined retirement bursting with beauty and new beginnings, wherein all the hardships of life are reconciled. He pictures himself seated in bliss, despite the many challenges of aging. May it be so, for him and for us all.

Reflections: Mu Soeng

The aspirations of the author of these verses touch upon some of our own aspirations. Especially in our retirement years, we long for a life of little complication, little involvement, and little stress. In other words, we become less ambitious toward outward gains and possessions and try to repurpose our lives toward the inner and the tranquil. The passions of yesteryears just don't have the same kind of pull anymore. We want to create our own metaphorical "cave" where we are protected from unwanted outside intrusions.

While this metaphorical cave is a natural human aspiration, its accomplishment is largely a matter of conditioning and self-corrections within that conditioning. We are all born into a matrix of greed, hatred, and delusion. To what degree we train ourselves to become free from the power of this matrix is a matter of self-correction. The author of these verses is hoping that becoming a wandering ascetic will be an answer to his "problems." It may have been a viable option for him at that particular time and place.

In ancient India both husband and wife might retire to a spiritual community in their "golden years" and use it as their metaphorical cave to be protected from the stresses related to the householder's life. I have spoken elsewhere of the possible model of an urban hermit for contemporary Buddhist practitioners (See Appendix B). The inspiration for the model is the possibility for all serious practitioners to repurpose and rearrange their lives according to the principles of living simply and dying joyfully, even while caring deeply for investigating one's own residual greed, hatred, and delusion.

I like to think that, through re-crafting our lives in our golden years, it is possible to aspire to the same sentiment that Tālaputa is hoping for. It is by no means going to be easy or comfortable—engaging seriously with deep meditation practice never is. It may perhaps have been even easier for someone in ancient India immersed in the ashrama model of attending to their golden years, but all human beings are capable of changing their lives at any time. Repurposing our lives will ultimately depend on our core aspirations: whether we truly want a life of serenity and psychological homelessness.

Reflections: Gloria Taraniya Ambrosia

Lately I have had many conversations with friends, family, and students who are approaching retirement age. This week alone I spoke with three people who have applied for retirement benefits and are evaluating the feasibility of letting go of virtually all worldly concerns in the interest of full-time spiritual practice … or something approaching that. Our lives may still be too complex for a cave in the wilderness, but one can always plan to simplify enough to make long retreats and/or a regular at-home formal practice routine possible.

The availability of various supports such as Medicare and Social Security (in the USA) couldn't be more timely. The body seems to be slowly breaking apart, and most likely will need medical attention in the coming years. Heck, it already does! By the time we reach 65, our energy levels and/or interest have diminished so that many retirees are less preoccupied with social and political issues. It's not that one is indifferent … it's just that through years of experience we've seen that these concerns are endless. Only the names and faces change. So perhaps it's time to leave such matters in the capable hands of the next generation. It's their turn. Instead, one can look forward to a steady diet of contemplation and meditation.

Interestingly, as energy levels decline, the wisdom factor matures to a point where we can begin to clearly see the machinations of self-concern for what they are—fabrications of a mind that has probably spent lifetimes in delusion. What relief one feels at the prospects of structuring a lifestyle that makes it possible to explore the nooks and

crannies of the mind with heightened interest and—dare I say—
understanding! It's time to LET GO and LET BE with greater vigor.

I'm just back from a two-month visit to the Western
monasteries in the lineage of Ajahn Chah. These monasteries are
filled with Western women and men—nuns and monks, laywomen
and laymen—who have been born and raised in similarly complex
cultures. The nuns and monks are people just like us who perhaps
responded to the call at a younger age and embarked wholeheartedly
on this spiritual path. Yes, they have suffered from the same
delusions, and even in monastic life have had to sort through the
same trivial battles that self-view sets up. But in an environment
that acknowledges basic ignorance without judgment, such battles
may be more easily seen for what they are, accepted, and probed.
We all have a long way to go, but living inside the monastery walls
can give one the sense that freedom is possible.

This is not a recruitment appeal for monastic life. One doesn't
want to romanticize that. It's more a tribute to the teachings and
practices of the Buddha. Whether we set out on the path when we
are young or when we are older, whether we have chosen to live
within a monastic community or in lay life, it is never too late to
practice for liberation. What older people may lack in energy, we
enjoy in wisdom and understanding. As lay people, we can draw
inspiration from the models that the Buddha established and use
our retirement years to establish a more contemplative lifestyle
so that we, too, can wholeheartedly focus on the middle way and
liberate the mind.

2. Equanimity

2.1 Beyond Joy and Sorrow

Upon a certain occasion, late at night when the Buddha was in seclusion, a certain minor *deva* named Kakuddha visited him with some questions. The following poetic exchange occurred:

Kakuddha: *Are you delighted, wanderer?*

Buddha: *What is it, friend, that I've received?*

Kakuddha: *Are you then grieving, wanderer?*

Buddha: *What is it, friend, that I have lost?*

Kakuddha: *Is it, then, wanderer, that you're*
Neither delighted nor grieving?

Buddha: *Friend—it is just so.*

Kakuddha: *I hope that you don't tremble, monk,*
Since no delight is to be found?
I hope that you can sit alone,
Without being consumed by regret?

Buddha: *Indeed I do not tremble, sprite,*
Since I'm consumed with no delight.
And so it is I sit alone,
Without being consumed by regret.

Kakuddha: *How is it you don't tremble, monk?*
How is it no delight is found?
How is it that you sit alone,
Without being consumed by regret?

Buddha: *Delight only follows distress;*
Distress only follows delight.
Neither delighted nor distressed,

> *Friend—this is how to know a monk.*

Kakuddha: *At long last I see a brahmin*
Whose fires are fully quenched; a monk,
Neither delighted nor distressed,
Who has traversed the world's attachments.
(Samyutta Nikāya 2:28)

Reflections: Andrew Olendzki

This is my hope for retirement—to have "traversed the world's attachments." This lovely poem describes a state of peaceful equanimity and contentment rooted in wisdom. Contentment is a state of mind and need not rely upon a particular set of external conditions. We are accustomed to thinking that we'll be content once this, that, or the other thing takes place, and we thereby put a lot of energy into trying to make those conditions manifest. Sometimes it works, and sometimes it doesn't. Even when it does, when we reach a goal (such as retirement) or fulfill certain criteria (such as having a comfortable place to live), it may still turn out that we are not content. Either the conditions change, as they are wont to do, or we find that new desires arise to clamor for our attention once the old ones are fulfilled.

At any given moment, the quality of one's experience will be defined by whatever emotional states are arising. Riding the roller coaster of desire, we might be gratified half the time and distressed the other half. We are being told by the Buddha, however, that we also have a third option—not climbing on board in the first place. Any moment with desire is a moment entangled in suffering. Any time we want things to be different than they are, we are setting ourselves up for disappointment. This is because delight and distress are two sides of the same coin, and we cannot have one without the other. It is precisely because he is not consumed with delight that the Buddha can "sit alone, without being consumed by regret."

36 • Older and Wiser

Many people will say it is worth the distress to experience the delight. As we mature, however, we may find ourselves drawn more to the middle range of experience, the state of mind described here by the Buddha in which the fires of desire no longer burn. This is of course the best-known metaphor for awakening: "the fires of greed, hatred, and delusion have been extinguished (*nirvāna*)." Conventional wisdom assumes it is boring and bland in this middle emotional range, but those who have experienced firsthand the equanimous quality of mind that comes from true mindfulness know better. Unencumbered by the emotional highs and lows, the mind is capable of a remarkable clarity and immediacy. Delight and distress do not spice up our experience as much as they confuse and obfuscate it.

If our contentment depends upon receiving the things that delight us or avoiding what causes distress, it will remain shallow. At the deeper end of the pool, the mind is more calm, more focused, and hence more powerful. Awareness itself is the most astonishing aspect of the human condition. As we learn to orient toward it more often and more skillfully, the contentment described here by the Buddha becomes increasingly accessible. Profound well-being awaits us here and now, in every moment, and can be reached simply by ceasing the attempt to get somewhere else.

Reflections: Mu Soeng

This dialogue seems to confirm a spectrum we find throughout the Buddha's teachings:

Middle Way = position of neutrality = neither delight nor distress = not clinging = ending of "selfing" processes = equanimity = quenching of fires = ending of suffering.

The "fires" in question are the desires to be and to have, in all their full-raging encroachments. Our entire human experience is shaped by these two sets of desires, either in crude forms or subtler indentations. This is our "unfinished" business.

Being bound neither by delight nor distress is a classical description of the mind-state of equanimity (*upekkha*). Bhikkhu Bodhi describes this mind-state as a "considering mind" ("because a prejudiced mind, a mind that has already been made up, cannot consider anything that is contrary to its accepted views"); a mind that has become pliable (*kammaniyā*); become stable (*thira*); become flexible (*mudubhūta*); reached a state of not fluttering (*anejapattā*). This is a concentrated mind (*samāhitta*), without blemish (*anāgana*), purified (*parisuddha*) and cleansed (*pariyodāta*) with all defiling tendencies gone (*vigatu-pakkilesa*).

This is admittedly an accomplishment of a buddha (with a small b) and a tall order for those not trained in the mental discipline. Still, in investigating deeply the workings of our own minds and meditative experiences, we may be able to catch a glimpse of some of the attributes described above. This glimpse, in turn, is a peek into the mind-state that has gone beyond [seeking] delight and [avoiding] distress.

I like the term "not fluttering" for describing what the Buddha is speaking of in this passage. This, obviously, is the fruit of practice. This "fruit" is not necessarily a neatly defined package, but rather a spectrum of its own where a practitioner can get a taste of "not-fluttering mind" and be inspired by it. It may therefore be useful to think of this spectrum as a path rather than some kind of end product. In that sense, walking this path is a kind of consilience for "traversing the world's attachments" as the passage says.

This consilience is especially helpful when we are confronted with issues of sickness, aging, and dying. The nineteenth-century Korean Zen Master, Kyong Ho, said, "Do not wish for perfect health; in wishing for perfect health, there is tremendous greed and wanting." In other words, a "considering mind," as described above, is stable enough to recognize that so long as we have this mind-body system there will always be some problem. We will get sick; we will get old; we will die. These are natural processes. Making peace with these natural processes requires an application

38 • Older and Wiser

of awareness and wisdom to our entire life, not simply our pursuit of happiness in the face of psychological suffering.

Kyong Ho also said, "Don't hope for a life without problems. An easy life results in a judgmental and lazy mind." Quite self-evident, don't you think?

Reflections: Gloria Taraniya Ambrosia

Reading this sutta my mind went right to the Buddha's teaching on the second noble truth, the cause of suffering. *Tanhā* is the movement of the mind that keeps taking exception to what is—wanting things to be another way (*bhava tanhā*), not wanting them to be the way they are (*vibhava tanhā*), or just being preoccupied with sensory experience (*kāma tanhā*), "relishing now here and now there," as the Buddha puts it. *Tanhā* is a restless agitation that makes it impossible to be content with things as they are.

Fortunately, we are practicing with the establishments of mindfulness. Over the months and years of practice—and the increasing capacity for non-attachment that this brings—we are gradually training the mind to override the deeply entrenched habits of craving and ignorance. Instead of being caught up in the to-ing and fro-ing of the unawakened mind, we are finding a place of peace in the presence of it. This represents a radical shift from how we usually relate to experience. Whether we realize it or not, by working with the establishments of mindfulness, we are developing an openhearted acceptance of the way things are … a simple contentment with what is.

This kind of openhearted acceptance doesn't happen overnight. We seem to have to go through the often painful process of seeing for ourselves that longing and resisting don't bring about the desired results. In fact, they only serve to lock us more tightly into the very behaviors we are trying to overcome.

Ajahn Chah said: "Practice to the point where you can't go forward, you can't go back, and you can't stand still. Then you will understand what it means to transcend suffering." The

Buddha knew this in a very profound way, as evidenced by his interaction with the *deva* Kakuddha. For us, waking up may play out in less remarkable ways, but we need to recognize and acknowledge the little ways that we are slowly getting free. We get inklings.

I was recently visiting one of my sisters. On Sunday morning we sat at her kitchen table enjoying our coffee and reading the paper. This was not an uncommon event for either of us, but what struck me was the fact that neither of us was drawn to the colorful pile of advertising inserts. Indeed, the entire pile had been unceremoniously cast aside, placed intact on the floor beside us. I glanced at the ad on top and noticed that Macy's was having a one-day sale … but even that didn't spark my interest … or hers.

Aging has its benefits. We begin to see through the lure of sense objects, to question the delight that they offer, and to feel the peace of not wanting. Granted, this shared experience with my sister did not represent the depth of peace enjoyed by the Buddha, but it felt liberating all the same. You might say it's the wisdom to know when enough is enough. Slowly, we are letting go of the world and discovering what it means to be content.

2.2 Sleeping Well

On one occasion the Buddha was dwelling at Ālavī on a heap of leaves spread out on a cow track in a *simsapā* grove. Then Hatthaka of Ālavī, while walking and wandering for exercise, saw the Buddha sitting there. He then approached the Buddha, paid homage to him, sat down to one side, and said to the Buddha: "Sir, did the Fortunate One sleep well?"

Yes, prince, I slept well. I am one of those in the world who sleep well."

> "But, Sir, the winter nights are cold.
> It is the eight-day interval, the time when frost descends.
> The ground trampled by the hooves of cattle is rough,
> the spread of leaves is thin, the leaves on the tree are sparse,
> the ochre robes leave one cold, and the gale wind blows cold."

"Well then, prince, I will question you about this matter. You should answer as you see fit. What do you think, prince?
A householder or a householder's son might have a house with a peaked roof, plastered inside and out, draft-free, with bolts fastened and shutters closed.
There he might have a couch spread with rugs, blankets, and covers, with an excellent covering of antelope hide, with a canopy above and red bolsters at both ends.
An oil lamp would be burning, and his four wives would serve him in extremely agreeable ways. What do you think, would he sleep well or not?"

> "He would sleep well, Sir. He would be one of those in the world who sleep well."

"But might there arise in that householder or householder's son bodily and mental fevers—

> born of greed,
> born of hatred,
> born of delusion
> —which would torment him so that he would sleep badly?"

"Yes, Sir."

"But a Buddha
    has abandoned such greed,
    has abandoned such hatred,
    has abandoned such delusion,
cut it off at the root, made it like a palm stump,
obliterated it so that it is no more subject to future arising.

Therefore I have slept well."

Indeed the sage who's fully quenched
Rests at ease in every way;
No sense desire adheres to him
Whose fires have cooled, deprived of fuel.

All attachments have been severed,
The heart has been led away from pain;
Tranquil, he rests with utmost ease.
The mind has found its way to peace.

(Anguttara Nikāya 3:34)

Reflections: Andrew Olendzki

Hatthaka assumes, as so many naturally do, that happiness and well-being depend upon material comforts alone. He is honestly perplexed when the Buddha tells him he has slept well outdoors on the ground, since as a prince he knows and understands only the life of pleasure and ease. Of course, the Buddha himself has been there and done that, abandoning the palace life to seek—and find—a deeper kind of happiness.

What use are all the worldly blessings, not only of a comfortable bed but also of youth, health, prestige, and wealth, if one's mind is not settled and roils with afflicted emotions? Is the image of twisting and turning sleeplessly in a comfortable bed really worse than that of sleeping contentedly on the hard ground? We have all observed for ourselves or heard stories about people who apparently have everything going for them and who yet burn with the fires of greed, hatred, and delusion. The stabbing arrow of always wanting and needing more, no matter what one already has acquired; the deadly poisons of discontent, envy, jealousy, bigotry,

42 • Older and Wiser

and distrust; the darkness of confusion, self-doubt, misguided views, and perverted perspectives—all these cause far more distress than a lumpy bed.

And what are the many losses and diminutions of age to those who are wise and deeply content, whose minds have found their way to peace? Of course, all things being equal, one would rather experience pleasure than pain, and of course chronic intense pain is disruptive to almost any sense of well-being. But surely the torments of the mind are ultimately harder to bear than those of the body. Some pain is an inevitable component of the human condition, but resisting that pain or resenting it or beating against it will only amplify it. One "leads the heart away from pain" by putting aside the struggle to optimize all conditions and adapting oneself instead to whatever is happening in the moment. One might still have human desires, but without clinging to them they "do not adhere."

In the poem above, the Buddha "rests at ease in every way" precisely because the fires (of greed, hatred, and delusion) have gone out. This is the very definition of *nibbāna* (*nirvāna*). It is not an escape from life, but a settling into it with tranquility, a resting in the world with utmost ease. We are far more equipped to understand this and to embody it when we are older. Only a young fool would hope to find happiness with four wives (substitute "partners" as appropriate). Taken literally or figuratively, it is an apt image of the futility of seeking to be "served in extremely agreeable ways," without from time to time being equally well served in extremely disagreeable ways.

The message of this story can be applied to many aspects of our lives. Contentment is an internal state which, at a certain stage of maturity and understanding, is not dependent upon outer conditions but upon inner health.

Reflections: Mu Soeng

Many years ago, even before I started formal Zen practice, I was, like many others at the time, deeply influenced by Carlos

Castaneda's books. Looking back, it seems I had enough discernment to be inspired by the "wisdom" content of these books rather than their drug experiences. One of the incidents narrated in the book made a huge impression and has remained with me ever since. In this incident, Castaneda and his teacher, don Juan, are wandering around in the high desert, when the night descends on them. They find a shelter among some cliffs and settle down to spend the night with the cliff wall against their back. Castaneda is very restless and cannot seem to settle down, while don Juan sits quietly even as his shadow merges with the night and he seems to become one with the night and the hills. An intrigued Castaneda asks about the secret of his tranquility, and don Juan says, "Nothing has been accomplished; yet nothing has remained undone. No need to struggle with anything. Just go back to your sleep."

In later years, these words spoke volumes to me when I came across the teaching of the perfection of this moment. This language of Zen was a mirror image of what don Juan was saying: this moment is perfect, just as it is. There's no need to change it in any way.

The dramatic setting of the conversation between Castaneda and don Juan seems to have been replicated in the dialogue between the Buddha and Hatthaka. What the Buddha is saying about sleeping well is the same admonition that don Juan gives to Castaneda: restlessness/not sleeping well comes from not being at ease with yourself. And, of course, not being at ease with yourself comes through the drives of greed or hatred or delusion. These drives, in turn, move the chariot of unwillingness to accept things just as they are.

The acceptance of things just as they are is not a passive condition, but rather a dynamic process where insight into the nature of things shines light on the fact that each moment is an encounter between the conditioned self and the phenomenon. The phenomenon itself is neutral: not good, not bad. As a Zen poem says,

>*Good and evil have no self-nature;*
>*Holy and unholy are empty names.*

Thus the problem lies entirely with the conditioned self, the conditioned mind, and how it is going to relate to inherently neutral phenomena. The above Zen poem is completed with these last two lines:

> *In front of the sense-door [the six senses] lies the door*
> *to stillness and light;*
> *Spring comes, the grass grows by itself.*

We may not pay much attention, but the grass growing by itself in the springtime is one of the greatest creative acts in the natural world. It can happen only because the grass is completely at ease with itself during its hibernation. At the same time, its emergence and growth is an entirely dynamic process. So too with the ability of the mind to train itself in the same manner.

Reflections: Gloria Taraniya Ambrosia

Hatthaka, a prince, is a bit miffed that the Buddha is able to rest so comfortably on a heap of leaves on a cow track, on the damp, uneven ground, with cold, gale-like winds blowing all around him. So am I. I would be a grumpy mess by morning! But that's exactly what makes this sutta so interesting. It points to the difference between an unawake worldling like me and a fully awakened being like the Buddha. What makes it possible for the Buddha to get a good night's sleep? He has abandoned greed, hatred, and delusion, cutting them off at the root so that they never arise again.

As Buddhist practitioners, we have all set ourselves the task of doing the same thing. If we're honest, though, most of us will admit that we thought it would be a tad easier. I expected complete liberation at some time during my first three-month retreat. I imagined bells and whistles and a flash of sudden awakening. "Then, boom!" I thought, "There will be no more greed, hatred, or delusion—no more suffering."

But it's not like that, is it? It's a gradual and sometimes brutally slow process of experiencing for ourselves both the harm and pain of these three unwholesome roots of suffering … and the great happiness and benefit of their wholesome opposites.

When we talk about overcoming greed, hatred, and delusion, we are talking about overcoming the ignorance at the heart of these. In the language of the four noble truths, we are talking about realizing right view and right thought—cleaning up the incorrect views, perspectives, and impulses that keep the unwholesome states vital in our hearts. The Buddha defines right view as understanding the four noble truths. Each of us goes through the process of understanding the suffering that is associated with craving … overcoming the ignorance at the root of it … directly experiencing its eradication … and developing the training that is the ticket out (*sīla, samādhi,* and *paññā*).

Our first seeing of the noble truths in their entirety is what brings about the breakthrough to the Dhamma. Once this vision is realized—the seeing of the noble truths—it is not yet liberation, but it is the opening up of the path to liberation. We have entered the stream and realized the first stage of awakening. There is then no place to go but all the way to freedom. One can never revert back to not knowing.

Right thought involves the systematic purification of the impulses that drive our actions by clearly seeing their *kammic* consequences. By applying ourselves in practice, we gradually see for ourselves the truth of the law of *kamma*—that skillful actions bring happy results and unskillful actions bring unhappy results.

Simply put, the combination of these two meditative insights—realizing the four noble truths and understanding the law of *kamma*—effects a way of being in the world that, in essence, trades greed, hatred, and delusion (or cruelty, as stated in the *suttas*) for renunciation, kindness, and harmlessness.

May we all trade greed, hatred, and delusion for renunciation, kindness, and harmlessness … and get a good night's sleep!

46 • Older and Wiser

2.3 The Single Most Precious Moment

One night, under the light of a bright full moon, the Buddha gave utterance to this poem, which he encouraged his followers to remember and to frequently ponder:

> *Do not chase after what is gone,*
> *Nor yearn for what is yet to be.*
> *For the past has been left behind,*
> *And the future cannot be reached.*
>
> *Those states that are before you now*
> *—Have insight into every one!*
> *Invincibly, unshakably,*
> *Know that well, again and again.*
>
> *Do this work today, with ardor;*
> *Who knows when death will come calling?*
> *There is no bargaining with Death,*
> *Or with his army of minions.*
>
> *Abiding ardently like this*
> *Without fail, both day and night, is*
> *"The single most precious moment."*
> *So the peaceful sage has told us.*

He goes on to give a detailed explanation of how these stanzas are to be understood:

> How does one not chase after what is gone?
>
> One does not nurture delight there thinking,
> 'I had such material form in the past,'
> 'I had such feeling in the past,'
> 'I had such perception in the past,'
> 'I had such formations in the past,'
> 'I had such consciousness in the past.'
>
> And how does one not yearn for what is yet to be?
> One does not nurture delight there thinking,

'May I have such material form in the future!'
'May I have such feeling in the future!'
'May I have such perception in the future!'
'May I have such formations in the future!'
'May I have such consciousness in the future!'

And how is one invincible in regard to states that are before you now?

Here, one does not regard:

- material form as self, or self as possessed of material form,
- or material form as in self, or self as in material form;
- feeling as self, or self as possessed of feeling,
- or feeling as in self, or self as in feeling;
- perception as self, or self as possessed of perception,
- or perception as in self, or self as in perception;
- formations as self, or self as possessed of formations,
- or formations as in self, or self as in formations;
- consciousness as self, or self as possessed of consciousness,

or consciousness as in self, or self as in consciousness;

On a later occasion, a group of monks approached the Elder Mahā Kaccāna and asked him to explicate the stanzas. His analysis was similar, but focused on the six sense bases rather than the five aggregates. The essential point remains the same: avoid having one's consciousness "bound up" with desire and craving for things that have passed, have not yet come, or are currently present.

(Majjhima Nikāya 131-4)

Reflections: Andrew Olendzki

This well-known poem drives home the theme of focusing one's mind upon the present moment. The mind so naturally swings like a pendulum, sweeping from the past and into the future while passing very quickly through the present. Especially as one gets older, it is common to dwell upon the past and to speculate about the future, often with some trepidation. The Buddha here reminds us that the present moment is a gift of inestimable value, and is our most precious possession.

The powers of the mind are seductive, insofar as we are capable of managing multiple affairs, recollecting all sorts of information, and speculating creatively about various future possibilities. Our ability to access, retain, and manipulate data is indeed impressive. But what we are missing as we do this is the potential depth of the present moment. When we extend the mind over a wide range of topics, it gets spread very thin; when we allow the mind to settle down upon a single experience, it gets deep and profound.

Elder years provide an opportunity to let go of the need to multitask and be productive, and instead cultivate a depth of consciousness that is our birthright. Just feeling the sun upon one's face or experiencing the body sitting comfortably without pain can be a moment of infinite wonder, boundless joy, and unfathomable profundity. We have the ability to focus upon the *quality* of consciousness, rather than upon its quantity or efficiency … and this is accessed by knowing the present moment very well.

The quality of consciousness is enhanced partly by the ability to focus the mind, without distraction, upon the arising and passing away of each moment's experience. This we do when we practice meditation. For the Buddha, the quality of consciousness also has to do with disentangling the mind from the toxic influence of desire and craving. As long as we are wanting something to be other than just what it is, part of our mental energy will be expended upon that wanting. In moments of mindful equanimity, however, the mind is freed up to place all of its resources upon an object without diminishment.

The primary ally of craving, and thus the main obstacle to mindful awareness, is the habit of taking everything personally, of viewing experience through the filter of "I, me, and mine." This is why we are told above to examine the present moment in ways that are not bound up with the construction of self. It is a challenge, to be sure, but the fruit of rising to that challenge is the experience of "a single most precious moment."

Just a word on the key phrase in this text. This is my own translation of the poem, and I am offering a new interpretation of its difficult penultimate phrase. Bhikkhu Ñāṇamoli called it "one fortunate attachment"; Bhikkhu Bodhi modified this to "a single excellent night"; and Ajahn Thanissaro renders it "an auspicious day." I'm taking the word *ratta* (night) in its more general sense of a period of time, which I think, given the context, can be construed as a present moment well encountered.

Reflections: Mu Soeng

The language and wording of this poem seem to have a Zen-like flavor, especially the lines *Do this work today, with ardor. Who knows when death will come calling?* Zen teachers often give a lion's roar of "this moment, this moment" to encourage students to bring their attention back to the koan they are working on, or to their *shikan-taza* practice.

I am also enchanted by the convergence between this poem and numerous other places where the Buddha spoke of letting go of the regrets of the past and letting go of worries about the future. I have often pointed out that the basic architecture of Buddha's teachings, specifically the second noble truth of the dependently-arisen nature of phenomena, speaks to the centrality of radical now-ness. Historians of Indian religions have called this approach of the Buddha "momentariness" (Pāli: *khana-vāda*; Skt: *kshana-vada*). Almost all Buddhist meditative traditions speak of moment-to-moment awareness. The current popularity of the term "mindfulness" also has this awareness of the present moment as its core principle.

But it also seems to me that this poem and its language are harkening us to a different orientation than our current understanding of mindfulness. There's a sense of urgency—the urgency to change—in this letting go of concerns with the past and the future because "Who knows when death will come calling?" My own Zen teacher used to exhort his students by saying, "You may die in five minutes. What can you do right now? When will you understand this great matter of life and death other than right now?"

The urgency to change is always changing the view and intention—the cognitive and the perceptual processes—as the basic wisdom architecture we bring to our practice. The call for the preciousness of this moment is always the call for transforming how we see or perceive the self and the world: changing the deeply conditioned habits of perceiving the mind-body as autonomous, permanent, and substantial, worth clinging to—to seeing it as a system with its own formations and structures that are always changing moment by moment. To be mindful, then, is to be in touch with this moment-by-moment change, without reference to past or future.

What the Zen tradition calls the "great work of life and death" is really a simplifying process: refining attentional capabilities to stay with the change happening in the present moment and eliminating all discursive thinking (which, after all, is no more than fantasy) about the past and the future. This elimination needs to be understood properly in its own context. It does not mean submitting to a fatalistic thinking, but instead really making a clear distinction between the functional and the speculative. If your roof is leaking, you need to arrange for a roofer to come and fix it. This planning about the future is purely functional. It does not involve thinking about the self or its past or its future.

On the other hand, constantly recreating a self in the events of the past or possibilities of the future is purely a speculative engagement, and an unwholesome one. In this poem, as in many other places, the Buddha is simply asking to eliminate this speculative thinking. This is the path to true happiness.

Reflections: Gloria Taraniya Ambrosia

One of the last things my father said to me before he died was, "Don't waste your energy rehashing what has been ... or imagining a brighter future. Be content with what you have and who you are." He was 74 at the time and, although he didn't know it, he was not long for this world. He had always been a practical man, apparently more interested in teaching my sisters and I how to get along in the world—how to lay tile or mow the lawn or conduct ourselves in the board room—than in encouraging us to contemplate the meaning of life. But now he bore the signs of someone who was worn out from years of wanting and striving. I remember thinking at the time that his words did not appear to be the empty musings of an aged father making one last pitch for the welfare of his daughter, but rather the thoughtful expression of something he had recently realized and wanted to share. And so this kernel of wisdom stayed with me.

Who knows the depth of what my father came to understand late in life? Still, I like to think that it was no different than what the Buddha is teaching here. In these four *suttas* from the *Majjhima Nikāya,* the Buddha is encouraging us to avoid "chasing after what is gone and yearning for what is yet to be," and to cultivate the right attitude toward the present. He is encouraging us to come to unshakeable peace through ardent and determined effort so that we might SEE arisen phenomena as they really are. The intended meaning is contemplation of the present moment without being misled into self-view by attaching to the five aggregates. Release from this attachment, which is the principle cause of our suffering, is no less than the realization of *nibbāna*, the highest happiness. Given the reality of death, what other enterprise could be more important?

Some say that as we age our attachments become more entrenched through years of repetition and delusion. Perhaps in some instances that is true, but for serious practitioners who are paying even just a little attention, there is also the very real possibility of learning to stand back from it all, to see body, feeling, perception, formations, and consciousness without identification. When we see beyond self, we no longer cling to these five aggregates as comprising who we are. And when we stop clinging, we enjoy peace.

For myself, I'm beginning to see aging as a blessing. I have moments wherein I forget what I am remembering. And it's increasingly difficult to get up a full head of steam of concern for the future. Collapsing time into the present is all one can seem to muster ... but one can't grasp after that either. Attachment takes too much energy!

I've been chewing on the words of my father for over 25 years now. With any luck, the wisdom of his simple message will find its way into my heart.

2.4 Two Ways to Prepare

Dhaniya:

"The rice is cooked,
my milking done.
I live with my people
along the banks of the Mahi;
my hut is roofed, my fire lit;
   so if you want, rain-god,
     go ahead & rain."

Buddha:

"Free from anger,
my stubbornness gone,
I live for one night
along the banks of the Mahi;
my hut's roof is open, my fire out:
   so if you want, rain-god,
     go ahead & rain."

Dhaniya:

"No mosquitoes or gadflies
are to be found.
The cows range in the marshy meadow
where the grasses flourish.
They could stand the rain if it came:
so if you want, rain-god,
go ahead & rain."

Buddha:

"A raft, well-made,
has been lashed together.
Having crossed over,
gone to the far shore,
I've subdued the flood.

54 • Older and Wiser

No need for a raft
is to be found:
so if you want, rain-god,
go ahead & rain."

Dhaniya:

"My wife is compliant, not careless,
is charming, has lived with me long.
I hear no evil about her at all:
so if you want, rain-god,
go ahead & rain."

Buddha:

"My mind is compliant, released,
has long been nurtured, well tamed.
No evil is to be found in me:
so if you want, rain-god,
go ahead & rain."

Dhaniya:

"I support myself on my earnings.
My sons live in harmony, free from disease.
I hear no evil about them at all:
so if you want, rain-god,
go ahead & rain."

Buddha:

"I'm in no one's employ.
I wander the whole world
on the reward [of my Awakening].
No need for earnings is to be found:
so if you want, rain-god,
go ahead & rain."

Dhaniya:

"There are cows, young bulls,

cows in calf, breeding cows,
& a great bull, the leader of the herd:
so if you want, rain-god,
go ahead & rain."

Buddha:

"There are no cows, no young bulls,
no cows in calf or breeding cows,
no great bull, the leader of the herd:
    so if you want, rain-god,
      go ahead & rain."

Dhaniya:

"The stakes are dug in, immovable.
The new muñja-grass halters, well-woven,
not even young bulls could break:
    so if you want, rain-god,
      go ahead & rain."

Buddha:

"Having broken my bonds
like a great bull,
like a great elephant
tearing a rotting vine,
I never again
will lie in the womb:
    so if you want, rain-god,
      go ahead & rain."

(Sutta Nipāta 18-29)

Reflections: Andrew Olendzki

This lovely poem employs a sort of call and response pattern that is common in the early Pāli texts. Each stanza uttered by Dhaniya is mirrored by the Buddha, using the same words but with a different meaning. The subtleties of the language cannot be entirely captured in translation, though Ajahn Thanissaro (whose translation this is taken from) does a good job of capturing the gist of it for us.

Two different approaches to life are contrasted here: that of the prosperous and fortunate householder who has arranged his affairs skillfully enough that he is ready for the rainy season to commence, and that of the wandering ascetic who has so removed himself from dependence upon outer conditions that no external change will interfere with his well-being. At every turn the householder is placing his trust in possessions and resources, while the Buddha is pointing again and again to a higher freedom accessible through no longer being dependent upon such things.

The fire in the first stanza, for example, means warmth and security for Dhaniya, while it is interpreted by the Buddha as the fire of greed, hatred, and delusion that burns within us. Having fully quenched that fire, the mechanisms that create suffering have come to an end for the Buddha. Dhaniya speaks of his wife as his steady companion in the fifth stanza, while the Buddha calls the mind one's constant companion. In his eyes, living with a well-ordered mind that is free of any unwholesome factors is even more of a comfort than an affectionate and virtuous partner.

The impending rains hang over the verses as something inevitable that can be prepared for in two different ways. In India the season gets very dry for many months, and then the rains come suddenly and dramatically. One can imagine everyone preparing for their onset in different ways, much like New Englanders prepare for the coming winter by gathering firewood and setting out snow shovels. This imagery can also be taken to convey the way one might prepare for the inevitable arrival of old age. Retirement involves putting affairs in order and planning for how one will cope with such things as diminishing health or mobility, the gradual loss of friends and loved ones, and how to face the larger existential issues concerning one's own mortality.

There is of course good sense in preparing for these things in practical ways, but there is a call in this poem to think about the matter in very different terms than we are accustomed to doing. Maybe we will be better off unburdening rather than accumulating, relinquishing rather than holding on, opening up to the radical contingency of our situation with trust and peace rather than trying to hold off and resist what we know deep down to be inevitable. The Buddha paints a picture of simple courage, of inner tranquility, of purifying the heart of qualities such as anger or stubbornness that cause fear and pain. It is a picture of freedom and a sense of well-being that is infinitely deep.

Reflections: Mu Soeng

This exchange between the Buddha and Dhaniya recalls that most fundamental of all questions: what can you ultimately depend upon? This ultimate dependence could also be translated as a "refuge," as in "What do you ultimately take refuge in?" A further parsing of this question may ask, "What can you depend upon when things are not going so well? What can you depend upon when things are going well?"

The Buddha often spoke of a "well-made mind" or a "well-trained mind" (*citta-sampanna*). In Buddha's teachings, a well-trained mind is the refuge for all seasons, whether it is the rainy season, summer, or winter. There's an unshakeable quality of equanimity in this well-trained mind.

Even the mosquitoes make their presence known in the poem above. The mosquitoes bother a Buddha/well-trained mind as much as they bother an ordinary person. The mosquitoes have no respect for what we think about or how we hold a certain conceptual view. They bother a philosopher of the first rank as much as they bother one of the third rank.

The mosquitoes here can be a metaphor for the ills of the body when it goes through sickness and aging. The mosquitoes are an integral part of an ecosystem in which all things (*dhamma*) of the phenomenal world move according to causes and conditions.

I am reminded of a particularly esoteric practice in one of the sub-schools in Japanese Shingon Buddhism wherein the monks go into the forest during the rainy season when mosquitoes are

58 • Older and Wiser

plentiful. Their practice is to sit motionless and let the mosquitoes bite as much as they can. As a result, they develop a level of tolerance to the extent that one more bite from the mosquito is not appreciably noticed. It may be medically true that this next bite does produce some pain, but this pain does not elicit a negative response. The practitioner gets to the point where even though some pain is felt, it does not destabilize the mind.

This esoteric practice has metaphorical value for dealing with our own processes of sickness and aging. If the mind is not well trained, it will react to even the slightest negative changes in the body (consider a teenager's obsession with his/her acne). Those of us in a certain age group have no choice but to deal with aches and pains in the body, as well as even more serious disabilities or bad medical news. What can we depend upon in this situation? Where do we find refuge? A well-trained mind understands that aging and sickness are integral aspects of the ecosystem of the body, and we can make peace with them just as the esoteric practitioner makes peace with mosquito bites.

Rather than positioning itself for passive acceptance of bad news, a well-trained mind can consider the situation to be dynamic and creative, and that there is enormous wisdom in the decline of the body. That is, it allows us to see the truth of *dukkha, anicca,* and *anattā* in more graphic ways than ever before. This truth-seeing then moves beyond the merely conceptual. It can now liberate the mind from its earlier conceptions of how the body should be, eventually opening us up to disenchantment and dispassion in positive ways.

Reflections: Gloria Taraniya Ambrosia

How do we prepare for our senior years? Like Dhaniya … many of us have prepared well. The bills are paid. We own the house. The kids are in reasonable shape. Everyone seems to be getting along. Medicare has kicked in. Our Social Security checks are arriving. Our financial advisor says the IRA and retirement annuity will carry us through. We're all set. Everything is nice and secure. Right?

It's certainly good to put our worldly affairs in order—to give attention to our so-called security. But this poem serves as a reminder that none of this guarantees our ultimate welfare … nor our liberation before we die. As both serious Buddhist practitioners and householders, we also want to turn our attention to our inner world. With the guidance of the Buddha, we do an internal weather report. How's our capacity to see the hindrances as they arise and to get a handle on these? Do we see the longing and resistance in the heart? Have we subdued the floods of *kilesā*, the fires of desire, the fetter of attachment? Is the mind tight or loose? Stubborn or malleable? Contracted and bound or kind and non-judgmental? Maybe our worldly affairs are in order, but do we clearly see that *anicca* (impermanence; transience), *dukkha,* and *anattā* (not-self; non-substantiality) still rule the day? Have we seen through the delusions that the unawakened mind sets up? And can we see these delusions with some semblance of regularity? Perhaps like Dhaniya we have prepared for every possible calamity, perhaps we have built great fences … but do we realize that none of that can really bring about ultimate happiness or prepare us for our inevitable demise?

As householders and Buddhist practitioners, our task is to juggle these contrasting objectives. We are not living the renunciate life wherein the requisites of food, clothing, shelter, and medicine are provided for us. One can reflect wisely on the brilliance of the Buddha in establishing an order of nuns and monks, thus giving the option of pursuing liberation unencumbered by worldly concerns. But as householders, we have not taken that option. So it's incumbent on us to eke out a lifestyle based in the world, but which nonetheless makes it possible for us to relate appropriately to that world—that is, without attachment. It's up to us to determine how to live within the complexities of Western culture and at the same time stride toward freedom.

Some say that for householders liberation is either impossible or extremely difficult. As the argument goes … we have to pay so much attention to worldly concerns that it is difficult to settle the mind enough to see clearly. But this has to be tested. Perhaps one of the blessings of living in Western culture is that for many

60 • Older and Wiser

of us it is possible to get our worldly affairs in order such that in our senior years we are freer to practice for liberation with greater interest and enthusiasm than ever before. Perhaps we are in better shape than we realize.

3. Aging

62 • Older and Wiser

3.1 The Lucidity of Age

Sāriputta, there are certain recluses and brahmins
whose doctrine and view is this:

> 'As long as this good man is still young,
> a black-haired young man
> endowed with the blessing of youth,
> in the prime of life,
> so long is he perfect in his lucid wisdom.

> But when this good man is old,
> aged, burdened with years,
> advanced in life, and come to the last stage,
> being eighty, ninety, or a hundred years old,
> then the lucidity of his wisdom is lost.'

<u>But it should not be regarded so.</u>

I am now old, aged, burdened with years,
advanced in life, and come to the last stage:
my years have turned eighty.
Sāriputta, even if you have to carry me about on a bed,
still there will be no change in the lucidity of the Tathāgata's
wisdom.

Rightly speaking, were it to be said of anyone:

> 'A being not subject to delusion has appeared in the
world
> > for the welfare and happiness of many,
> > out of compassion for the world,
> > for the good, welfare, and happiness of gods and
humans,'
> > it is of me indeed that rightly speaking this should be said.

(Mahā Sīhanāda Sutta, Majjhima Nikāya 12)

Reflections: Andrew Olendzki

Conventional wisdom tells us that our senior years are a period of inevitable mental decline. The Buddha here tells us this need not be true. Who are you going to believe?

It is true that certain physical afflictions have an effect on how well our mind works, and if something goes wrong with the hardware of the brain, it is bound to have an effect upon its software and operating system. Such things can occur at any age, however, and are not specific to the aging process. Plenty of younger people get knocked on the head, forget what they were going to say, or otherwise get dazed or confused from time to time. (I seem to recall quite a few such episodes late on a weekend night when I was in college.)

I think some of the attitudes on this subject come from unreflective assumptions that the mind is reducible to matter, and must therefore diminish as the physical body loses some of its functionality. Yet though it depends upon it in many ways, the mind is not identical with the brain. Many recent studies have shown that as some parts of the brain get injured or cease to work well, mental activity is re-routed in quite astonishing ways. Some people are able to heal from certain kinds of stroke, by-passing the damaged areas and carving out new neural pathways. The whole visual cortex can be "borrowed" by other senses when higher-level visual processing is impaired, allowing people to "see" with their sense of touch or other mental resources.

For decades we have been well aware of how the brain affects the mind, but new research in neuroplasticity is demonstrating how the mind is effecting changes in the brain as well. Not surprisingly, some of this research comes from the study of mindfulness. In one well-reported study, Sara Lazar (*Neuroscience* 2005) has shown not only that the left pre-frontal cortex of experienced meditators thickens significantly, but also that the natural thinning of this same area that often comes with age is inhibited in those who meditate often.

I think this is what the Buddha was talking about in the *Lion's Roar Discourse* all those years ago. His mind was lucid at eighty years old not because he was a special being that had come into the world, but because he was mindful at all times. He was a man who was born in this world, aged, became ill, and eventually passed away like everyone else. It is the practice of mindfulness that accounts for the Buddha's resistance to delusion, just as it was mindfulness that allowed him to "see things as they really are" and become awakened.

The more we allow our minds to lapse into habitual patterns of response, living on autopilot, as it were, the more it is likely to constrict. But in mindfulness we have, if not an elixir of life, a way of using the mind that holds out the promise of keeping it lucid to the very end.

Reflections: Mu Soeng

Two phrases from this passage speak to me as complementary and mutually-informing, like the yin-yang symbol from Chinese Taoism. The first one is "lucid wisdom" or "lucidity of wisdom"; the second is "a being not subject to delusion."

It seems to me that the Buddha here is making an inherent connection between wisdom and delusion. On the face of it, the setting suggests that some people, the recluses and the Brahmins, were privileging youth and young age. This is understandable within the context of shramana (the wandering ascetics) culture against which all religious contestings and truth-claims took place. The ascetic practices were indeed a young man's game. The Buddha himself was a young man when he left home to enter the forest and take up ascetic practices. His own practice was extreme enough to make him stand out as a champion ascetic. However, we of course know that this kind of asceticism did not gain him the wisdom he was seeking. So he tweaked the system and found a middle way between extreme asceticism and sensual indulgence.

This was part of his learning curve: extreme asceticism did not necessarily bring wisdom. In this passage, there seems to be another learning curve: acquisition of wisdom has nothing to do with age. The correlate to acquisition of wisdom is the power of delusion. Delusion also is not confined to any particular age group; young people can be as deluded as older people.

When the Buddha speaks of the Tathāgata as the one who is not subject to delusion, we have a clear marker of what wisdom means, and its correlate of what practice means. There also seems to be the question of "backsliding" here: the wisdom of the Tathāgata is unshakeable even in the face of getting old.

It may be the case that practitioners make breakthroughs in practice in their youth, but may lose the pristine quality of that breakthrough as they encounter old age. That's why the Buddha advocated "seclusion" as a way of protecting one's mind. I have known Zen masters in their eighties and nineties who followed this advice and were embodiments of not losing their insight and wisdom.

The nuance that emerges for me from this passage is that if a person who is now in his/her senior years but has practiced for many years, chances are they have had insights into the workings of their own mind/conditioning and have had enough glimpses into the nature of phenomena to see its inherent impermanence and insubstantiality. As a result, they will hopefully no longer seek contentment in external phenomena. Or, at least, they have weakened delusion enough so that when it does arise there is enough residue of wisdom left from earlier cultivation to stop them in their tracks, take a deep breath, and start a fresh round of inquiry.

This is how I see the benefit of getting older—that one is able to stop in their tracks before they spin out too much in their own stories—that they are able to return to the "refuge" their practice has created for them within themselves and regroup in a wholesome and wise manner.

Reflections: Gloria Taraniya Ambrosia

When traveling in other countries, we often come face-to-face with deeply engrained cultural attitudes we didn't even know we held. Obviously, this door swings both ways: we discover biases and perceptions that we have about others ... and we see how others perceive us. Through everyday situations, we often experience incongruities or discrepancies between how we view ourselves and how others see us.

A number of years ago I was travelling in Thailand with one of the nuns in our lineage, serving as her attendant as we visited monasteries in the northeast. Stepping down from the bus that carried us from Bangkok to Phu Wieng, Khon Kaen province, we were greeted by three young Thai women who had come to collect us. They bowed to Sister, which was to be expected. But then they turned to me, knelt before me with hands in *anjali* (a posture of respect), and all but tossed rose petals at my feet as we moved toward the waiting car! This kind of deferential treatment continued throughout our stay. When I asked why I was being treated with such care, it was made clear to me that it was because of my age—most obviously signified by my white hair. Clearly, the Thais have mastered the art of respect for elders.

Needless to say, however, I was stunned ... and saddened, too ... as I realized that, in America, I had become increasingly accustomed to feeling invisible and even ignored as I age. And yet I know that I am better than I have ever been—wiser, more confident and authentic, with much more to offer.

On a mundane level this sutta serves as a reminder of how wrong we can be when we measure a person's worth based on age ... with youth assuming the more valued position. And yet it's a very common attitude in our culture. I think it behooves us to give some thought to how we might turn this around. One isn't advocating a seniors' rights movement ... just more clarity internally in our hearts and externally in our communities as to our worth. I think this needs to be acknowledged and addressed because it is hurting us as a society, let alone as individuals.

Having said that ... to suggest that this sutta is only about giving senior citizens their due would completely miss the profundity of what the Buddha is pointing to. His was not ordinary wisdom. Rather, he had realized penetrating insight into the nature of reality and unbounded compassion that manifests as an unparalleled willingness to offer what he knows to others.

The Buddha is pointing to the optimal level of wisdom and compassion that is possible in this human experience, a level that transcends body and mind. Once we realize that level of wisdom, nothing … not even a weakened, decrepit, or dying body can take it away. Even sickness, aging, and death are no threat to the liberated mind.

3.2 The Worldly Winds

It is among misfortunes
that one's steadfastness is to be known,
and this only after a long time, not casually,
by one who is attentive, not by one who is inattentive,
and by one who is wise, not by one who is unwise.

Here a certain person,
being beset by the loss of a relative, or
being beset by the loss of wealth, or
being beset by the loss of health,
would reflect thus:

"That's the way it is
for one living in the world,
that's the way it is
for one who has taken on becoming a self."

When one is living in the world,
when one has taken on becoming a self,
eight worldly things
turn along with the world,
and the world turns along
with eight worldly things:

gain and loss;
fame and infamy;
praise and blame;
pleasure and pain.

Being beset by the loss of a relative, or
being beset by the loss of wealth, or
being beset by the loss of health,

one does not grieve,
one does not get worn out,
one does not lament,
one does not clamor, beating one's breast,
one does not fall into despair.   *(Anguttara Nikaya 4:192)*

Reflections: Andrew Olendzki

It is natural to encounter misfortunes, and the longer one lives, the more inevitable these become. The teaching offered here by the Buddha encourages us to remain steadfast amidst these reversals of fortune rather than allowing ourselves to be broken by them. This is not a matter of closing ourselves off from experience, even from painful experiences, but of learning not to be swept away by them in unhealthy ways. This approach combines opening up to the implacability of the natural order (such as Skinny Gotami learned to do in *The Mustard Seed, #6.2*) and avoiding stabbing oneself with a second arrow (as discussed in *Stabbed by One Arrow—Not Two, #4.2*).

Sometimes referred to as the eight worldly winds, the four pairs of favorable and unfavorable circumstances listed here serve as a backdrop to the human condition. This is just what it means to be human; this is just what each of us is sure to encounter every day in small and large ways; this is just the way it is "for one who has taken on becoming a self." This wonderful phrase refers to being born into this world in the first place, but more subtly means becoming a self each and every moment as we favor some things and oppose others. The pushing away of what we don't like and the pulling toward us what we crave is itself what constructs the sense of self, and once we have taken on this way of responding, it is unavoidable that some things will gratify us while other things cause us dismay.

Since sometimes you win and sometimes you lose, sometimes you're a hero and sometimes a chump, sometimes people like you and sometimes they don't, and because sometimes things feel good and sometimes they feel terrible—you are guaranteed to suffer if you do not widen your view to encompass it all. The Buddha is teaching us here how to roll with things rather than resist them, to adapt, adjust, and accept what happens while retaining a sense of equilibrium.

It is important to understand the words being used here for 'grieve' (*socati*), 'get worn out' (*kilamati*), 'lament' (*paridevati*), and the rest. These are all terms referring to greed- or hatred-based emotional responses—not terms referring to mental pain. Of course, one feels sorrow with the loss of a loved one, but we are being pointed toward a kind of 'pure' sorrow that experiences mental pain without the augmentation of self-referential emotional turmoil. We feel the sting of one arrow (the feeling tone of sadness), even very deeply, but do not amplify and multiply the pain by repeatedly stabbing ourselves with a second arrow (emotional responses such as resisting the feeling, yearning for something different, or taking it all personally).

We are not meant to feel good about the bad things that happen to us, but to accept that such things do happen regardless of our wishes. When we put them in perspective in this way, they will not have the power to defeat us. Adjusting ourselves to the inevitable rather than yearning for the impossible is a skill that can be learned. It allows us to feel deeply without being thrown into despair.

Reflections: Mu Soeng

Most cultures have some kind of folk wisdom that says, "Adversity tests your character," or "Adversity builds character," or something like that. The first few lines of this poem seem to be pointing to the same axiom. When these lines talk about the steadfastness of one who is attentive or one who is wise, they seem to be talking about "character" in their own way.

One of the tenets of Existentialist philosophy is that life is a struggle. The first noble truth of *dukkha* also seems to speak to that struggle. The eightfold path is a response to this struggle: how to train oneself in being steadfast, in being attentive, in being wise/mindful. I had not thought earlier about the quality of steadfastness in connection with the eightfold path, but after reading these lines, it hit me in the face. Yes, steadfastness is what it is all about. Zen masters admonish their students, "Above all, do not wobble."

Life presents all kinds of difficulties all the time. How do we train ourselves in not wobbling, in remaining steadfast, not as some kind of fake existential posture but through a deepening of *sīla*, *samādhi*, and *paññā?*

I was once at a Zen temple up in the mountains of Korea when a bus arrived loaded with Koreans and some travelling Americans. A Korean husband and wife, perhaps in their late fifties, was part of this group. These two were long-time students of my Korean teacher, and they both seemed in perfectly good health and good cheer. Their son was in fact the driver of the bus they were traveling on. We hiked up the mountain to the temple in the early morning to take part in a big ceremony. Since I was in robes at the time, I was invited to partake in the ceremonial lunch along with perhaps a hundred other monks. Before I went into the lunch, I was talking to the husband along with a few other people, and everything seemed fine. When I came out of the lunch, about an hour later, I was told that this man, the husband, had died. It sounded like a bizarre joke, and I tried to make sure I had understood correctly. I was told that this man was sitting on the floor against the wall, talking to others, when he said that he was feeling a bit sleepy and was going to lie down. He then slid down and never woke up!

Even more extraordinary was that the wife and son, obviously in shock, were not freaking out. They continued to say how grateful they were that the husband and father had died on the temple grounds surrounded by so many monks, and so on. Regardless, their sense of equilibrium in the face of their immense and sudden loss was quite moving. It was also a lesson in cultural training: in Korea people are very aware of their public behavior and how it impacts other people. In any case, I would like to hope that the wife and son were steeped enough in Buddha's teachings of not becoming a self that they could deal with their loss in a balanced way.

Dealing with the eight worldly conditions of gain and loss; fame and infamy; praise and blame; pleasure and pain is the texture of our existential lives, especially in a complex society. We deal with these things both internally and externally, and it seems to me that if there is a seamlessness between the internal and the external in our responses to these eight worldly conditions, then that's what the Buddha would mean by being attentive and wise.

Reflections: Gloria Taraniya Ambrosia

Reading this sutta selection, I immediately recalled an incident a number of years ago when I was living in Raleigh. A neighbor asked me to come down to her apartment. She was very sad and upset and needed someone to talk to. I can't recall the details of her difficulty, but I remember that I did what we often do in such situations—I problem-solved, tried to fix the conditions of her life, tried to find a way to make the realities of life more palatable, tried to find a way out. I wanted to offer her something useful to make her feel better, and so I struggled to find words to comfort her—all of which, by the way, was lovely. But after a number of false attempts I could see that, while there are certainly times when these kinds of offerings bring comfort, this time they offered little relief.

The exasperation of the moment finally overcame me, and I just threw up my hands and said, "I don't know about this crazy life. If it isn't one thing, it's another. We have a few moments of happiness, then we're entrenched in pain. Now we're up, now we're down. One day everybody likes us, the next day we're eating worms. That seems to be what's going on here, and I just don't know what to say to you to make that any different or better."

Well, that did it. My neighbor stopped mid-sob and burst out laughing! We were both overcome by what was, to this day, one of the best belly laughs we've ever had. We laughed so long and hard that we couldn't catch our breath. We touched the truth of what it is like to get caught up in the worldly winds and, for the moment, we broke the pattern. Instantly, the whole problem—neither one of us can even remember what it was—evaporated. To this day, that moment ranks among one of the most real and present moments of my life.

This teaching, while both basic and simple, is nonetheless profound in that it challenges us to see things differently. It challenges us to get under the apparent realities of the world.

The eight worldly *dhammas*—praise and blame, gain and loss, happiness and unhappiness, fame and ill-repute—guide or direct our lives until or unless we learn to settle down beneath appearances into the deeper reality of things. It's as if the Buddha is guiding us to stop getting caught up in the emotion of the moment and to look more closely at what is taking place— to see how what we are experiencing keeps changing and how we are affected by this changeability. In doing so, we gain direct personal knowledge of the nature of reality. Used wisely, this teaching is a way of getting to that kind of realization—finding the calm in the midst of turmoil, finding the truth beneath appearances. Lose the clinging to appearances, and we lose the anxiety associated with living in the world and becoming a self.

3.3 The Monk and the King

An elderly king of the Kurus, Koravya by name, goes to see
the venerable Raṭṭhapāla, a wealthy local youth who has gone
forth into the Buddha's community and become a bhikkhu. The
king says that most people go forth into the homeless life as a
response to aging, illness, loss of wealth, or the loss of relatives.
Yet none of these factors seem to apply to him, so why has
Master Raṭṭhapāla gone forth? He responds:

Great king, there are four summaries of the Dhamma that have
been taught by the Buddha who knows and sees, accomplished
and fully enlightened. Knowing and seeing and hearing them, I
went forth from the home life into homelessness. What are the
four?

(1) 'Life in any world is unstable, it is swept away.'

> How should the meaning of that statement be
> understood? [asks the king]

What do you think, great king? When you were twenty or
twenty-five years old, were you an expert rider of elephants,
an expert horseman, an expert charioteer, an expert archer, an
expert swordsman, strong in thighs and arms, sturdy, capable in
battle?

> When I was twenty or twenty-five years old, [I was
> indeed all these things]. Sometimes I wonder if I had
> supernormal power then. I do not see anyone who
> could equal me in strength."

What do you think, great king? Are you now as strong in thighs
and arms, as sturdy and as capable in battle?

> No. Now I am old, aged, burdened with years, advanced
> in life, come to the last stage; my years have turned
> eighty. Sometimes I mean to put my foot here and I put
> my foot somewhere else.

Great king, it was on account of this that the Buddha who knows and sees, accomplished and fully enlightened, said: 'Life in any world is unstable, it is swept away.'

(2) 'Life in any world has no shelter and no protector.'

> But, Master Raṭṭhapāla, there exist in this court elephant troops and cavalry and chariot troops and infantry, which will serve to subdue any threats to us. How should the meaning of that statement be understood?

What do you think, great king? Do you have any chronic ailment?

> I have a chronic wind ailment. Sometimes my friends and companions, kinsmen and relatives, stand around me, thinking: 'Now King Koravya is about to die, now King Koravya is about to die!'

What do you think, great king? Can you command your friends and companions, your kinsmen and relatives: 'Come, my good friends and companions, my kinsmen and relatives. All of you present share this painful feeling so that I may feel less pain'? Or do you have to feel that pain yourself alone?

> I cannot command my friends and companions, my kinsmen and relatives thus. I have to feel that pain alone.

Great king, it was on account of this that the Buddha who knows and sees, accomplished and fully enlightened, said: 'Life in any world has no shelter and no protector.'

(3) 'Life in any world has nothing of its own; one has to leave all and pass on.'

> Master Raṭṭhapāla, there exist in this court abundant gold coins and bullion stored away in vaults and lofts. How should the meaning of that statement be understood?

What do you think, great king? You now enjoy yourself provided and endowed with the five cords of sensual pleasure, but will you be able to have it of the life to come: 'Let me likewise enjoy myself provided and endowed with these same five cords of sensual pleasure'? Or will others take over this property, while you will have to pass on according to your actions?"

> I cannot have it thus of the life to come. On the contrary, others will take over this property while I shall have to pass on according to my actions.

Great king, it was on account of this that the Buddha who knows and sees, accomplished and fully enlightened, said: 'Life in any world has nothing of its own; one has to leave all and pass on.'

(4) 'Life in any world is incomplete, insatiate, the slave of craving.' How should the meaning of that statement be understood?

What do you think, great king? Do you reign over the rich Kuru country?

> Yes, Master Raṭṭhapāla, I do.

What do you think, great king? Suppose a trustworthy and reliable man came to you from the east [west, north, south] and said: 'Please know, great king, that I have come from the east [west, north, south], and there I saw a large country, powerful and rich, very populous and crowded with people. There are plenty of elephant troops there, plenty of cavalry, chariot troops, and infantry; there is plenty of ivory there, and plenty of gold coins and bullion both unworked and worked, and plenty of women for wives. With your present forces you can conquer it. Conquer it then, great king.' What would you do?

> We would conquer it and reign over it.

Great king, it was on account of this that the Blessed One who knows and sees, accomplished and fully enlightened, said: 'Life in any world is incomplete, insatiate, the slave of craving.'

> "It is wonderful, Master Raṭṭhapāla, it is marvelous [said the king] how well that has been expressed by the Buddha who knows and sees, accomplished and fully enlightened. It is indeed so!"

(Raṭṭhapāla Sutta, Majjhima Nikāya 82)

Reflections: Andrew Olendzki

It is an interesting historical note that some people were seen to go forth into the homeless life in ancient India on account of aging or loss, since we also have many examples of young people, including the Buddha himself, entering into the contemplative life. Of course, the primary reason one goes forth into retirement is aging, although this can also happen because of illness or loss of employment. Whatever the cause of beginning one's retirement phase of life, we can allow ourselves to be guided by the Buddha here in regard to what can continue to motivate us during retirement.

He is pointing toward something more primal than the ordinary conditions of life. In the first case he invites the king to reflect directly on his own experience: Do you remember how vital and capable you once were? And do you notice what it feels like to now be so reduced compared with that? There is a great existential truth in knowing and seeing this so viscerally. The instability of it all, the fact that everything vital does eventually diminish and vanish, is a noble truth about the way things really are: *dukkha*. I think it is poignant that the king does not understand the second and third point, since he has an army to protect him and abundant treasures to sustain him. But of course the troops cannot protect him against illness, and he cannot retain ownership of the treasure beyond this life. The fourth point is probably the more illuminating one for the king to learn, because Raṭṭhapāla points out that his own desires are boundless. Like a bull before the cape, he cannot help but want to conquer everything he can. Notice the wording: because one is a slave to craving, this world will always—by definition—be incomplete.

Raṭṭhapāla was inspired by the Buddha to go forth into the contemplative life, not because there will be some sort of magical alleviation of these four challenges, but because he could learn to find contentment and well-being even in the face of them. Those who have truly gone forth relinquish their hold on possessions (and the hold possessions have upon them), surrender to the inevitabilities wrought by impermanence, and work to abandon the deep-seated

78 • Older and Wiser

craving that makes these things a problem. By "surrender" I do not mean giving up and allowing oneself to be overwhelmed by change, but rather no longer struggling against what is inevitable. If you stand in one place and resist a flowing river, you will be battered by its current; if you give in and remain in place, you will be drowned by it; but if you no longer resist and learn to move with what is happening, you are carried downstream but can remain afloat and in harmony with the waters that surround you.

This might be overdoing the metaphor somewhat, but as I understand what the Buddha is offering by going forth, it is the ability to be peaceful and at ease in the midst of the core instability of the world. Raṭṭhapāla gets it, but will the king?

Reflections: Mu Soeng

These four statements from Raṭṭhapāla, attributed to the Buddha, are what I would call the DNA of Buddhist thought and practice: (1) 'Life in any world is unstable, it is swept away.' (2) 'Life in any world has no shelter and no protector.' (3) 'Life in any world has nothing of its own; one has to leave all and pass on.' (4) 'Life in any world is incomplete, insatiate, the slave of craving.'

In the passage above, we see how the monk is trying to explain each of these statements to the king, and it is not difficult to imagine that each of us might be able to interpret them in useful language. But it is more difficult to imagine the world being this way when we are young. What is being offered here is a vision of the core instability of the world. When we are young, we are locked into a way of perceiving the world as inherently stable, and we imagine it as our playground, much as a painter sees an empty canvas.

The interesting subtext here is that the king, now an old man of eighty, has never thought of the world in this way and, furthermore, he cannot understand how Raṭṭhapāla, a formerly-privileged young man, can think of the world in this way. It is not only a tremendous perceptual learning curve for the king, but also an emotional jolt.

Fast forward to our own situation, and imagine your teenage son or daughter coming to you and wanting to talk about these four statements. Chances are you are in your forties or early fifties, and you have imagined the world to be a certain way all these years. If you are honest with yourself, you would secretly hope that your son or daughter has simply read too many "corrupting" books or seen too many depressing European movies, and that he or she will "grow out" of it.

It is a hard and painful process to reimagine the basic shape of things other than how we have been conditioned to imagine them to be. We have been conditioned to put our trust in a certain organizational order and structure in which things move in a certain way to find their logical place in the scheme of things. In our contemporary culture, it is practically taboo to think of disorder, of chaos, or even unhappiness or alienation.

It is also practically taboo that young people should think of old age, of dying, of things falling apart. They may read William Butler Yeats: "Things fall apart; the centre cannot hold;/ Mere anarchy is loosed upon the world, / The blood-dimmed tide is loosed, and everywhere/ The ceremony of innocence is drowned;/ The best lack all conviction, while the worst/ Are full of passionate intensity." But when they bring these sorts of thoughts home, they disturb the "convictions" of their parents and their elders.

In this passage, Raṭṭhapāla is saying to the king that he left home at a young age because he became convinced of the disorder and the chaos of the world that the Buddha was teaching (chances are he would have been supported by his family and culture in his decision to leave home), while the king is still struggling with his convictions about his own life and his perceptions of the world. It is a delicious conversation and to be savored by each of us in our own way.

Reflections: Gloria Taraniya Ambrosia

Earlier today I was talking with someone who is having difficulty facing the reality of death. She's not ill, but she's getting older and she finds that with each passing year the anxiety is building. As she put it ... she has read all the books, listened to all the Dhamma talks, volunteers at Hospice, and reads every how-to article in AARP in order to get a handle on her fear and depression. But she finds that none of these activities make her feel better about the fact that she's going to die.

I found our conversation very timely in that I've been contemplating this sutta on the monk and the king. My friend is on the right track. She is facing the divine messengers—aging, sickness, and the inevitability of her own demise. Yes, these preliminary sparks of awakening can be scary. But we can also celebrate our good fortune ... that we have lived long enough for these realities to become so apparent. For much of our lives—especially in our youth—our common response to these might have been to deny, turn away, wish it would be otherwise, or simply ignore them altogether. At some point, however, these get our attention and we begin to contemplate our lot as human beings. We might read the books and listen to the talks, as my friend noted, in an effort to sort it all out. This is all good, but it only constitutes a preliminary right view—one that is enough to get us going more deliberately on the path toward liberating insight.

Gradually ... and over time ... we go beyond opening to sickness, aging, and death and become interested in the deeper truths from which these proceed. That's what Ratthapāla has done. Listening to the Buddha, he realized the impermanent, unsatisfactory, and selfless nature of our existence, and this became the profound insight that moved him to take up the holy life—even at a young age. Through his conversation with the king, Ratthapāla skillfully explains how to use direct experience to do what he did ... to reflect beyond appearances. Youth is gone. There is no protection from illness. No matter how great our bank account, it is limited in that we can't take it with us when we die. And if we follow the path of looking for happiness through acquisition … all we do is cultivate more wanting. We are never satisfied.

As human beings, we are highly conditioned to survive at all costs. Be secure; be certain. Avoid pain; ensure pleasure. Be in control; be on top of things. But the Buddha's teachings challenge us to confront this instinctive response to conditions. We have to touch our helplessness in the face of *anicca, dukkha,* and *anattā* and make peace with that. The mind might go bonkers. We can watch how it wiggles and squirms. But sooner or later it comes around to the fact that it's better to accept life on its terms than to constantly be at odds with it. Then the fact that we are all going to die becomes more palatable.

3.4 Getting Near the End

During the rains the Buddha was attacked by a severe sickness,
with sharp pains as if he were about to die.
But he endured all this mindfully,
clearly aware and without complaining ...

Then the Buddha, having recovered from his sickness,
as soon as he felt better, went outside
and sat on a prepared seat in front of his dwelling.

Then the Venerable Ānanda came to him,
saluted him, sat down to one side and said:

"Lord, I have seen the Buddha in comfort,
and I have seen the lord's patient enduring.
And, Sir, my body was like a drunkard's.
I lost my bearings and things were unclear to me
because of the Buddha's sickness ..."

[The Buddha replied:]
Ānanda, I am now old, worn out, venerable,
one who has traversed life's path.
I have reached the term of life, which is eighty.

Just as an old cart
is made to go by being held together with straps,
so the Tathāgata's body
is kept going by being strapped up.

It is only when the Tathāgata
withdraws his attention from outward signs,
and by the cessation of certain feelings
enters into the signless concentration of mind,
that his body knows comfort.

Therefore, Ānanda,
you should live as islands unto yourselves,
being your own refuge,

with no one else as your refuge,
with the Dhamma as an island,
with the Dhamma as your refuge,
with no other refuge.

And how [does one do this]?

Here, Ānanda, a person abides contemplating

- the body as body ...
- feeling as feeling ...
- mind as mind ...
- mind-objects as mind-objects

earnestly, clearly aware, mindful,
having put away all hankering and fretting for the world.

(Parinibbāna Sutta, Dīgha Nikāya 16)

Reflections: Andrew Olendzki

There is a lot going on in this passage of interest to those of us who are getting older. The first is the simple recognition that the Buddha (also referred to here as the Tathāgata, an epithet) was human, and as such it was natural that his body would age, become ill, and eventually die. He speaks poignantly of these things, and in the last weeks of his life he reminds Ānanda on several occasions that all things change and pass away.

Another important fact revealed here is that the Buddha experienced intense pain toward the end of his life. His awakening was not about the cessation of pain, but the cessation of suffering, which is not the same thing. We tend to conflate the two, but feeling tones of pleasure and pain are an intrinsic element of the mind/body system, while the experience of suffering only occurs as an optional and unskillful emotional reaction to these feeling tones. When pain is approached "mindfully, clearly aware" it becomes a sensation to be investigated rather than an affliction to be resisted, a response that only amplifies it.

It is also interesting to hear the Buddha say that feelings of physical pain subside only when he enters states of advanced concentration. One can't help but wonder if he did so as an escape from the pain, which does not seem to align with his mindful endurance of the pain without suffering. But I read this passage as a simple description of the facts, not as him advocating that one should practice *jhāna* (absorption) to avoid pain, or as him admitting that he fled to *jhāna* for refuge from the pain. Matter of factly: pain is here. Equally matter of factly: in concentrated states it is gone (the *jhāna* formulas in the texts specify how feeling tones gradually subside as one progresses through the stages of concentration).

On the literary front, we cannot help but be moved, first by Ānanda's expression of sympathy and compassion in the face of his master's illness, and then by the Buddha's description of his body as an old cart, made to go by being held together with straps. I'm not yet as old as eighty, but I'm beginning to get the sense, sometimes first thing in the morning and sometimes at the end of a busy week, of what he may be referring to.

The final passage in this exchange is an important one, and has been the source of some misunderstanding. We sometimes find it rendered "Live as lamps unto yourselves," or even "Be a lamp unto yourself," which yields a very different meaning. The ambiguity stems from the fact that two different words in Pāli (lamp, island) share the same spelling. It seems clear from the context, however, that his point is not that one should follow one's own sense of what is true, but rather that one can use mindfulness as a refuge from pain and affliction. It is not only concentrated states that offer relief, then, but also the equanimity of mindfulness practice. By keeping awareness closely focused on the four foundations of mindfulness, rather than elaborating upon and proliferating about what is happening, those of us who may not yet be at the Buddha's stage of development can find shelter from the storm of affliction. In moments when we might need it most, this can be a tremendous blessing.

Reflections: Mu Soeng

There's a story of a young man who comes to a Zen monastery and wishes to be admitted into the training program. He tells the supervising teacher that he is a sincere person looking for a cure for his anxiety problems. He says that he is willing to practice very diligently but wants some reassurance that his anxiety problems will disappear. The teacher tells him there is no guarantee in these things and therefore no reassurance can be given. The frustrated young man asks, "What then is the point of this practice?" The teacher replies, "This training is to prepare yourself to meet the moment of your death. This much assurance can be given: if you do things properly, you will meet the moment of your death with courage and dignity."

I find echoes of this exchange in the story of Buddha's last days. When the time came for his body to fall apart, the Buddha handled his dying moment as a living testimony to how training in equanimity, in non-clinging, in acceptance of things as they are had been done for 45 years before that moment. The point of the Zen story as well as the dying moment of the Buddha seems to be the last line of the text, "having put away all hankering and fretting for the world."

Even though the Buddha is able to enter into a deep *jhāna* state as a way of coping with intense physical pain, he continues to point toward the much larger issue of non-clinging. "Living your life as an island," and "Be a refuge unto yourself," require a lifelong training in self-sufficiency that has its analog in putting away "all hankering and fretting for the world."

An interesting subtext for me in both stories—the young man coming to the monastery, and the life of the Buddha—is that they both started their training in their early years. As we know, the dying moment of the Buddha was preceded by 45 years of intense self-discipline (plus six years of extreme asceticism before that). In our vernacular, he had "put his life on the line" in training himself. It is only through his training and self-discipline that he was able to meet the moment of death in the way that he did.

The point then is that we cannot simply think or talk ourselves into dealing with intense physical pain or sickness or the overwhelming certainty of death lurking around the corner. Such a relief will not come through a coffeehouse discussion about the dharma. We need to put our lives on the line, too … in a metaphorical sense, of course.

Reflections: Gloria Taraniya Ambrosia

In this excerpt from the *Parinibbāna Sutta,* we see a sharp contrast between how the Buddha and Ānanda addressed suffering. The Buddha enjoyed relief from his pain through the signless concentration of the mind. (One might also imagine that even when not absorbed he was able to endure his physical pain without mental distress.) By contrast, during this last great illness of the Buddha before his ultimate demise we see Ānanda going to pieces. By his own admission, he "lost his bearings" and forgot everything he knew. Seeing this, the Buddha appealed to Ānanda … and to us … to take refuge in the Dhamma by earnestly contemplating the four establishments of mindfulness.

No manner of wishing that things would be otherwise can alter the fact of suffering. We study and practice and learn about letting go. But when the chips are down, when it's time to face our own grave sickness or that of a loved one … how will we meet it? Will it be with or without attachment? With or without delusion? The only way to ensure some semblance of peace in such moments is to apply ourselves to this liberating practice while we still can.

Through the establishments of mindfulness, we become familiar with the distinct aspects of experience—body, feeling, mind—and learn to leave it at that. We break through identification with the body and mind and know them in a more simple and direct way. Through this increasing non-identification, we experience an interesting paradox. No longer attached to the tendency to DO something about what is happening … or to react to it … we connect more fully with the experience itself. Non-attachment cuts through the tendency to quarrel with what is. Gradually we develop the capacity to let things be. Even sharp pains can be known without attachment.

When it comes to being at peace with sickness, aging, and death, probably most of us will admit to having a long way to go. It's only been in the last few years that I find my heart opening more fully to sickness. And my Dhamma buddy and I freely admit that it has taken every bit of ten years to open to and accept the increasing signs of aging. As to being at peace with death … I wailed when my parents died fifteen and twenty-five years ago. Indeed, to a bystander I probably appeared to have lost my bearings. But despite my pain, I know I wasn't wallowing. Rather, I was practicing wholeheartedly to turn toward the painful arisings in my heart and to ride the waves of sorrow without attachment. I was endeavoring to be with what was happening—to feel it in my body, to open to the feeling tone, to do my best not to resist or ignore it—in short, to let death be. Without the benefits of practicing with the four establishments of mindfulness, the loss of my parents might well have been unbearable.

I am confident that with continuing effort in practice we can all grow in our capacity to know what it is like to abide "contemplating the body as body … feeling as feeling … mind as mind … mind-objects as mind-objects … earnestly, clearly aware, mindful, having put away all hankering and fretting for the world." May it be so.

4. Illness

4.1 Afflicted in Body—Not in Mind

On one occasion the householder Nakulapitā
approached the Buddha, paid homage to him,
sat down to one side, and said to him:

"I am old, venerable sir, aged, burdened with years,
advanced in life, come to the last stage, afflicted in body, often ill
Let the Buddha exhort me, let him instruct me,
since that would lead to my welfare and happiness for a long
time."

So it is, householder, so it is!
This body of yours is afflicted, weighed down, encumbered.
If anyone carrying around this body were to claim to be healthy
even for a moment, what is that due to other than foolishness?

Therefore you should train yourself thus:
'Even though I am afflicted in body, my mind will be unafflicted.'

1. How is one afflicted in body and afflicted in mind?

Here an uninstructed person ... unskilled
and undisciplined in the Dhamma of the noble ones:

Regards **form** as self, or self as possessing **form,**
or **form** as in self, or self as in **form.**
He lives obsessed by the notions:
'I am **form, form** is mine.'

As he lives obsessed by these notions,
that **form** of his changes and alters.
With the change and alteration of **form,**
there arise in him sorrow, lamentation, pain, displeasure, and
despair.

[The same is said of **feeling, perception, volitional formations,**
and **consciousness.**]

2. And how is one afflicted in body but not afflicted in mind?
Here the instructed noble disciple ... skilled

and disciplined in the Dhamma of the noble ones:

Does not regard **form** as self, or self as possessing **form**,
or **form** as in self, or self as in **form**.
He does not live obsessed by the notions:
'I am **form**, **form** is mine.'

As he lives unobsessed by these notions,
that **form** of his changes and alters.
With the change and alteration of **form**,
there do not arise in him sorrow, lamentation, pain, displeasure, and despair.

[The same is said of **feeling, perception, volitional formations, and consciousness**.]

(Samyutta Nikāya 22:1)

Reflections: Andrew Olendzki

The first thing to strike us about this passage is, once again, the Buddha's searing honesty about the realities of aging. It is the very nature of all material things to break down, and for one whose body is advanced in years this is plainly evident and foolish to deny. (Interesting how common such denials are in our own society. It would be almost rude to reply to such speech as Nakulapitā with anything other than "Oh, not at all; you look great!")

The second thing we might expect to hear is something about the incorruptible soul within the body. Many traditions, both east and west, consider the body to be just a temporary vessel to carry the soul, which is fundamentally immune from decay. But in early Buddhist teachings, the mind is as conditioned and interdependently arisen as the body, so the diminution of the mind is a very real possibility. The Buddha's advice to Nakulapitā is very practical and rooted in compassion: Care must be taken to attend to the health and well-being of the mind.

The way to do this is through a third unexpected element in this text, for the Buddha is not talking about the conventional health of the mind, which might be addressed through good nutrition or memorization exercises, but rather the deeper existential health of non-attachment. We are all afflicted in mind, regardless of our age, if we take our body, our pleasures and pains, our ideas and perceptions, our emotional patterns, or our consciousness to constitute a truly existing entity called the self. It is so easy to assume that these five aggregates "belong" to me or are "contained" in me somehow (the "me" being something that stands outside the aggregates) or that I am something like a homunculus (a little person) that resides within the aggregates. All these views of the self involve some sort of attachment, and are thus a source of affliction.

The problem with such identifications is that when something changes—which it is sure to do, often—then I will inevitably suffer "sorrow, lamentation, pain, displeasure, and despair." The sense of "I" is a strategy for preserving stability in an ocean of change, so when the changes it is expected to protect against do occur, then it becomes a catastrophe. The defense against this that the Buddha seems to be offering Nakulapitā is to not take it all personally, to not entangle the body and mind by projecting ownership upon them.

By doing so we gain more than we lose. We can still be very mentally aware of what is happening, but instead of this mental energy going into, "Oh, no! Look what's happening to me!" it manifests more as, "Look at what is happening here— isn't it interesting!" That slight deflection, where one looks at something as an interested observer rather than as one heavily invested in one particular outcome (in this case, in the outcome that nothing changes for the worse in my mind and body), makes a world of difference to our well-being and is the epitome of mindfulness. Seeing things as they actually are, rather than as we wish them to be, is ultimately our greatest ally as we age.

Reflections: Mu Soeng

Among the various teachings of the Buddha on the perils of aging and sickness, this one is as elegant (and graphic) as they come. Remember, among the four sightings the future Buddha had prior to his leaving home to go into the forest, one is of an old man, decrepit and bent at the waist. When the alarmed young man asked his charioteer if it will happen to him, too, the reply was yes … it happens to everyone. So we can all resonate with the householder Nakulapitā's plight. It's not that monks don't go through the same process; they just might not complain about it in the same way.

The exchange begins with Nakulapitā asking for a teaching, "since that would lead to my welfare and happiness for a long time." We can consider this to be standard literary rhetoric in ancient Buddhist texts, but it could also be the case that the householder is saying that he is still enamored of his aging and afflicted body and, rather than becoming disinterested in maintaining it for a long time, as monks are supposed to train for, he still wants the Buddha to "make it better." Consider how often we go to a doctor asking to be rid of this or that affliction, wanting to be made better so that we may continue enjoying ourselves.

Buddha's response: "If anyone carrying around *this* body were to claim to be healthy even for a moment, what is that due to other than foolishness?" can be read both at a local level and at a meta-level. Nakulapitā's aging and afflicted body is the local frame of reference, but all bodies at all times are a meta-perspective on the plight of the human body. We learn from the biological sciences that the human body stops growing at the end of our teenage years. In common medical understanding, the male body stops growing when the epiphyseal bone plates are completely sealed between the ages of 18 and 21 years old; the female body stops growing around the age of 18. From then on it is a matter of the homeostasis (an exquisite evolutionary system in itself) being maintained at an optimal level until it meets middle age. It is a fateful and poignant encounter—fateful because of the warning signal that the system is running out of steam, poignant because so few accept its inevitability.

One way of reading what the Buddha is saying is that the human body, after a few precious years of youth, is always in a stage of losing ground at the cellular level. It is precisely so because the body (*rūpa*) is a construction (Pāli: *sankhāra*; medical: homeostasis) and, as such, subject to various stresses and pressures. How can a person trained in the wisdom of *anicca* and *anattā* depend on this construction as a source of lasting happiness?

So the idea of "making it better" does not work in the long run. Or does it? It seems the Buddha is saying that the *nāma rūpa* (form, feelings, perceptions, formations, consciousness) cannot be made better at a biological or cellular level. But one can train oneself to accept, emotionally and psychologically, its ups and downs as natural happenings—to fix when something is fixable, but not to expect a miracle.

Reflections: Gloria Taraniya Ambrosia

On my first reading of this sutta I recalled a tender exchange I had with my mother many years ago. Standing beside her in front of the mirrored medicine cabinet, I watched as she put on her make-up. She was taking great care to paint the eyeliner just right. Suddenly she turned to me and said, "I look at this wrinkled, old face and it just doesn't feel like it's me." I could tell it was a source of pain for her—as if she either didn't understand or couldn't accept the changes taking place in her body. In my clumsy effort to offer relief, I laughed and blurted out a much too flippant response, "THAT should tell you that you aren't your body!"

Her puzzled look told me that wasn't the most helpful response, but I just let the moment pass. Still … the sentiment of the exchange lingered. In a few simple words my mom had captured one of the riddles of this human birth … and her eyes revealed the pain of trying to sort it out.

We dwell in this body and mind, but who are we really? If we think we are form, feeling, perception, volitional formations, and consciousness, we cling to experience at these levels and thus live life swinging on a pendulum. When the body looks good or feels good, "I" feel good. When the body is old or afflicted, the mind is distressed. The constant volley between pleasure and pain, between agreeable and disagreeable views or mental states, alternately delights and upsets us. We think well or ill of ourselves. It's all so exhausting!

In their search for relief, some people try to control the body and capture eternal youth. Some repress disagreeable thoughts or ideas and try to make everything appear happy or safe. Some resist the changing tides of the body and mind and get more and more depressed as the years go by. The Buddha's advice to the householder Nakulapitā reminds us to snap out of these extremes. "The noble disciple ... does not regard form, feeling, perception, volitional formations, and consciousness as self, etc." Thus, we avoid the sorrow that accompanies attachment, and when these five aggregates change, as they necessarily do, the "mind will not be affected."

It sounds so simple, doesn't it? It's a prescription for mental health. And yet realizing this depth of non-attachment may be years or lifetimes in the making. Fortunately, our moment-to-moment task remains as simple and accessible as it was on the first day of our first meditation retreat. Relax, pay attention, and hold experience lightly. See if you can notice the subtle movements of the mind grasping at sensation, feeling, and thought. Feel the pain of doing that. And then don't forget to notice the happiness of release.

4.2 Stabbed by One Arrow—Not Two

An uninstructed person feels a pleasant feeling, a painful feeling, and a feeling that is neither-painful-nor-pleasant. An instructed noble disciple also feels a pleasant feeling, a painful feeling, and a feeling that is neither-painful-nor-pleasant. What is the difference between an instructed noble disciple and an uninstructed person?

When an uninstructed person is in contact with a painful feeling, he sorrows, grieves, and laments; he weeps beating his breast and becomes distraught. He feels two feelings—a bodily one and a mental one. It is just like when a man is struck with an arrow, and then is struck again immediately afterwards with a second arrow: the man would feel a feeling caused by two arrows. So, too, when the uninstructed person is in contact with a painful feeling ... he feels two feelings—a bodily one and a mental one.

- When in contact with a painful feeling, one harbors aversion towards it. When one harbors aversion towards painful feeling, **the underlying tendency to aversion** towards painful feeling lies behind this.

- When in contact with that same painful feeling, one seeks delight in sensual pleasure. For what reason? Because the uninstructed person does not know of any escape from painful feeling other than sensual pleasure. When one seeks delight in sensual pleasure, **the underlying tendency to lust** for pleasant feeling lies behind this.

- When one does not understand as it really is the origin and the passing away, the gratification, the danger, and the escape in the case of these feelings, **the underlying tendency to ignorance** in regard to neither-painful-nor-pleasant feeling lies behind this.

If one feels a pleasant feeling, one feels it attached. If one feels a painful feeling, one feels it attached. If one feels a neither-painful-nor-pleasant feeling, one feels it attached. This is called an uninstructed person who is attached to birth, aging, and death; who is attached to sorrow, lamentation, pain, displeasure, and despair; who is attached to suffering, I say.

When an instructed noble disciple is in contact with a painful feeling, he does not sorrow, grieve, or lament; he does not weep beating his breast and become distraught. He feels one feeling—a bodily one, not a mental one. It is just like when a man is struck with an arrow, but then is not struck again immediately afterwards with a second arrow: the man would feel a feeling caused by one arrow only. So too, when the instructed noble disciple is in contact with a painful feeling ... he feels one feeling—a bodily one, not a mental one.

If one feels a pleasant feeling, one feels it unattached. If one feels a painful feeling, one feels it unattached. If one feels a neither-painful-nor-pleasant feeling, one feels it unattached. This is called a noble disciple who is unattached to birth, aging, and death; who is unattached to sorrow, lamentation, pain, displeasure, and despair; who is unattached to suffering, I say.

This is the difference between an instructed noble disciple and an uninstructed person.

> *For one who's heard much and comprehends dhamma,*
> *Who clearly sees both this world and beyond it,*
> *Desirable things do not churn up his mind,*
> *For the undesirable—no aversion comes.*
>
> *Neither attraction nor repulsion for him:*
> *They're calmed, gone to rest, and no longer exist.*
> *Knowing the state without sorrow, without flaw,*
> *One understands well, gone beyond becoming.*
>
> (Samyutta Nikāya 36:6)

Reflections: Andrew Olendzki

This text is the presumed origin of the well-known modern aphorism, "Pain is inevitable, but suffering is optional." It points out the extent to which much of the suffering we experience is self-inflicted.

The arrow metaphor demonstrates this graphically in regard to physical pain, which many of us face more often as we age, and which we all face when we are ill. Such pain, in the Buddhist teaching, is an inherent aspect of the human condition. The *dhamma* is not promising to take away the pains associated with a physical body, but it does teach how to find well-being even in the face of pain. The mindful approach to treating chronic pain involves turning toward the primary sensations and paying close attention to their texture, rather than trying to block them out or resist them. Indeed, much of the discomfort of pain turns out to reside in secondary responses to the primary sensations, such as tensing the muscles or catastrophizing anticipated experiences. Stabbing ourselves with the second arrow only makes things worse.

The same dynamic applies to psychological pain. There is nothing we can do about what comes up in the mind in response to various situations, for the conditions governing the arising of fear, or anxiety, or anger, or grief have been laid down in the past. The Buddhists call this karma, while we might give it such labels as learned behaviors, conditioned responses, or habituation. But we do have some influence on how we respond to what comes up. Once an emotion has arisen, we have the option to respond to it either skillfully or unskillfully. The Buddha is telling us that it is unskillful and unhealthy (words derived from the same root) to stab ourselves with a second arrow by judging ourselves, blaming ourselves, or otherwise trying to invite or refuse particular experiences.

Built in to the human psyche at a very primitive level are the underlying tendencies toward greed, hatred, and delusion (given slightly different labels in this text). The question that comes up every moment is whether these will be evoked, reinforced, and augmented by our responses to experience, or whether we allow them to atrophy by choosing instead to cultivate their opposites: generosity, kindness, and wisdom. Every time we have aversion toward what is unpleasant or crave for something more pleasant to arise, we are strengthening the underlying tendencies that give rise to suffering. The alternative is counterintuitive but ultimately healthier: accept the inevitability of discomfort when necessary, try not to constantly wish things were other than they are, even when they are difficult, and seek ways of finding contentment that do not depend entirely on pleasant sensations.

As the verses associated with this passage indicate, one can pass beyond the need for experience to become one thing or another, to become other than it is, by gradually diminishing and eventually extinguishing the reflexive tendency toward attraction and repulsion. Whatever it is—let it be. Resistance does not help, but will only make it hurt more.

Reflections: Mu Soeng

The eminent Korean Zen master Bojo Chinul (1158-1210) often said that the only difference between saints and ordinary people is that the former can control their minds while the latter cannot. This passage makes the same distinction between the uninstructed and the instructed person.

So when an uninstructed person comes into contact with a painful feeling, he "makes" something: "... he sorrows, grieves, and laments; he weeps beating his breast and becomes distraught." Similarly, when he comes into contact with a pleasant feeling, he "makes" something: he rejoices, he gloats, he dances around, and so on. In both cases, the "making" is taking the pleasant or the unpleasant feeling "personally." This is the wedge that opens up the Buddha's teachings into the entire spectrum of our life. We live our lives by taking things personally. We take our feelings, our emotions, our ideas, our opinions, our thoughts personally; we claim ownership of the painful and the pleasurable. In taking these feelings personally, we "make" I, me, mine, which then turn into the emotional-cognitive nodes through which our daily lives are lived.

I am reminded of the wonderful phrase, which is the title of

Ajahn Sumedho's book, "Don't Take Your Life Personally." Just this title seems to be a complete teaching in itself.

As the passage makes clear, the only difference between an uninstructed and an instructed person is that while both feel the physical pain in equal measure, the former allows himself to claim ownership of the event and thus engender a psychological component that is not engendered in the latter.

In so many words, this passage is also about how *papañca* (proliferation) works. In the passage here, an uninstructed person proliferates a second (mental) arrow after being struck by the first (physical) arrow, whereas the instructed person does not. Both feel the physical pain, but one proliferates, the other does not.

This habit of *papañca*-making has tremendous consequences. All our conditioning conspires to egg us on to indulge in proliferations. It is not only the second hit of the mental arrow, but also a third hit of still another layer of mental sorrow coming out of proliferation, and a fourth, and a fifth, and ad infinitum until we are confused and lost in the maze. The instructed person, on the other hand, stays calm and abides in a mind that remains "unchurned," as the passage says. He or she does not proliferate beyond experiencing the physical pain.

If we extend this habit of *papañca*-making to the processes of our later years, we see that encountering sickness or aging with aversion leads us to proliferate a construct: "I am a sick person," or "I am an old person." It may be that some of the aversion toward sickness and aging is inevitable, but it is also possible to take great care in how we proliferate our awareness of them. Is it possible to train ourselves and observe, "This body is sick," or "This body is getting old"? It may be that such training will lead one to not proliferate a hit of the second arrow. It may be that it all comes down to what story we tell ourselves about the first arrow. How and what story is told will determine the difference between the first and the second arrow, and the difference between a "saint" and an ordinary person.

Reflections: Gloria Taraniya Ambrosia

This teaching on the second arrow is often one of the first teachings we hear as fledgling Buddhists … and, I dare say, one that seals our attraction to the teachings. With this down-to-earth metaphor, the Buddha directs us to see for ourselves that our experience of pleasure, pain, and neither is distinct from the reflexive and seemingly inevitable responses of wanting, resisting, and ignoring that follow.

This may not sound like much, but as "uninstructed" people, we often find ourselves at the mercy of our own reactivity. Our minds are not settled with the reality of pain, and so we go on and on about it. We tend to compound difficulty by, in effect, having something to say about it, trying to fix it, change it, or make it go away. As the sutta says, "One feels it attached." For many of us … much of the time … this is where we live. The Buddha is trying to get us to see this and to stop being tied to mental patterns that masquerade as remedies for difficulty, but that only serve to lock us into useless reactions and behaviors. With study and practice, we begin to look in the right places for "remedies" and for freedom.

This sutta describes that freedom. What's left when we stop longing, resisting, or ignoring the experience of feeling? We become "a noble disciple who is unattached to birth, aging, and death; who is unattached to sorrow, lamentation, pain, displeasure, and despair; who is unattached to suffering." In other words, we find ourselves living more fully with the reality of the first noble truth.

This is not easily won, is it? Opening to a pain in the knee is one thing, but opening to the full reality of *dukkha* is quite another matter. When my brother-in-law died a few weeks ago it threw the whole family into a tailspin. It was so sudden, and we all thought he was too young and too full of life. Like Cunda when Sāriputta died or Ānanda when the Buddha died, we lost our bearings, we resisted, we didn't want it to be true. How can this be? How can Dave be gone?

I wrote to a monk friend and told him I hate the first noble truth. I said that it's hard to remember the other noble truths when I'm caught in the thick of the first. "Insight into *dukkha* isn't any fun at all!" I wrote. "Facing the reality of death," he replied, "is when the Buddha's truth smacks us between the eyes." But in the next sentence he also reminded me that the Middle Way leads to knowledge and understanding. It's the way out. It's the real remedy. We side-step the extremes and settle down between the habits of longing and resisting.

> *Neither attraction nor repulsion for him:*
> *They're calmed, gone to rest, and no longer exist.*

With *sati*, we remember the Middle Way. We let feeling BE feeling and thus avoid being pierced by the second arrow.

4.3 Healing Wounds

Suppose a man were wounded by an arrow
thickly smeared with poison,
and his friends and companions,
his kinsmen and relatives,
brought a surgeon.

The surgeon would cut around
the opening of the wound with a knife,
then he would probe for the arrow with a probe,
then he would pull out the arrow
and would expel the poisonous humour
without leaving a trace of it behind.

Knowing that no trace was left behold, he would say:
'Good man, the arrow has been pulled out from you;
the poisonous humour has been expelled
with no trace left behind,
and it is incapable of harming you.

Eat only suitable food;
do not eat unsuitable food
or else the wound may suppurate.
From time to time wash the wound
and from time to time anoint its opening,
so that pus and blood do not cover the opening of the wound.
Do not walk around in the wind and sun
or else dust and dirt may infect the opening of the wound.

Take care of your wound, good man,
and see to it that the wound heals.'

The man would think:
'The arrow has been pulled out from me;
the poisonous humour has been expelled
with no trace left behind,
and it is incapable of harming me.'

He would eat only suitable food,
and the wound would not suppurate.
From time to time he would wash the wound
and from time to time he would anoint its opening,
and pus and blood would not cover the opening of the wound.
He would not walk around in the wind and sun,
and dust and dirt would not infect the opening of the wound.

He would take care of his wound
and would see to it that the wound heals.

Then, both because he does what is suitable
and because no trace was left behind
when the foul poisonous humour was expelled,
the wound would heal,
and because it had healed and was covered with skin,
he would not incur death or deadly suffering.

So too, it is possible that some bhikkhu here might think thus:
'Craving has been called an arrow by the Buddha;
the poisonous humour of ignorance
is spread about by desire, lust, and ill will.
That arrow of craving has been pulled out from me;
the poisonous humour of ignorance has been expelled.
I am one who is completely intent on *nibbāna.*'

Being one who really is completely intent on *nibbāna,*
he would not pursue those things
unsuitable for one completely intent on *nibbāna.*
He would not pursue:

- unsuitable forms with the eye,
- unsuitable sounds with the ear,
- unsuitable odors with the nose,
- unsuitable flavors with the tongue,
- unsuitable tangibles with the body, or
- unsuitable mind-objects with the mind.

Because he does not pursue [these things],
lust does not invade his mind.
Because his mind is not invaded by lust,

he would not incur death or deadly suffering.

I have given this simile
in order to convey a meaning.
This is the meaning here:
'Wound' is a term for the six internal bases.
'Poisonous humour' is a term for ignorance.
'Arrow' is a term for craving.
'Probe' is a term for mindfulness.
'Knife' is a term for noble wisdom.
'Surgeon' is a term for the Tathāgata,
the Accomplished One, the Fully Enlightened One.
(Sunakkhatta Sutta, Majjhima Nikāya 105)

Reflections: Andrew Olendzki

Here is one of the places in the early Buddhist literature where the Buddha identifies himself as a physician or healer, in this case playing the role of a surgeon who treats a wound. The physical metaphor is standing in for a much deeper healing of the psyche, in which one needs to cleanse the mind of the toxin of ignorance in order to be truly well.

As we age, we are more likely to face medical interventions of one sort or another, and it is helpful to have a positive image such as this on hand to counteract the generally negative connotations of surgery. Yes, it is a shame to have to cut into the body, and it seems such an act of violence and intrusion, but when the scalpel is wielded by a true healer, the cutting away of what ails us is a benevolent act. While probing into an open wound is painful, and extracting an arrow even more so, the short term discomfort is in the service of long term well-being.

Mindfulness is identified as the probe, and becoming closely aware of our experience often uncovers what is difficult and even painful. It hurts to see clearly, to expose the toxins at work deep in our minds. But the goal of Buddhist practice is transformation, not ease. Rooting out what causes harm and then cutting it away once and for all with the scalpel of wisdom is a crucial step in any program of real and lasting healing.

Notice also, however, that one is not suddenly restored with the arising of wisdom, but that one's insights need to be carefully tended and protected. The behavior of the patient, as with our own conduct in the world, is an important component of deep healing. Avoiding the harmful effects of "unsuitable" sensory experience is compared with protecting against the corrupting effects of dust and dirt to a healing wound.

Ultimately the cure is in a healthy lifestyle, including good eating habits, good hygiene, and an attitude of caring for oneself in a wholesome way. Applying the physical metaphor to the mental, we need to use wise attention in regard to the things we see, hear, smell, taste, touch, and think about, recognizing that some things are healthy and others are not. We need to "wash" our minds from time to time with the clear waters of awareness, perhaps laced with loving kindness and equanimity, and guard against the ossifying influence of adherence to views and opinions. In short, to paraphrase the *sutta*, one needs to take care of one's mind and see to it that the mind heals.

As powerful as the field of medicine has become, with its astonishing new surgical technologies, a more significant field of preventative medicine has emerged, very much influenced by the practice of mindfulness and Buddhist images of well-being. Just as greater maturity helps us understand and accept a more holistic view of physical health, perhaps it can inspire us to apply this metaphor of healing to our mental, emotional, and moral life as well.

Reflections: Mu Soeng

These days, the phrase "self-healing" has become synonymous with what the Buddha called "healing the wound," with its own particular technologies and approaches. Self-healing is, for example, the ultimate phase in Gestalt Therapy. In its broadest sense, self-healing is a recovery from psychological trauma, as well as the automatic, homeostatic processes of the body that may correspond to structural misalignments.

More recently, the "mind-body connection," made popular by Herbert Benson and a forerunner of the Mindfulness-Based Stress Reduction movement, has used meditation as a self-healing mechanism for decrease in stress hormones in chronic states, improvement in anger and other negative emotions, and preventing DNA damage.

It is only more recently that the influence of Buddha's approach to meditation has been recognized as one of the earliest empirical approaches to self-healing. This particular passage lends itself organically to our current perspectives on self-healing, but it also goes beyond to the largely civilizational aspects of self-healing an entire culture.

Thus, when the Buddha says that craving is the cause of ignorance which, in turn, spreads greed, hatred, and delusion (and that walking on the path to *nibbāna* is facilitated only by the "pulling out the arrow of craving") he is speaking in a very wide sense—not only of personal healing, but also the healing of humankind.

All beings everywhere are pierced by the arrow of craving and infected with the poison of greed, hatred, and delusion. These arrows in turn compel people to create social and political systems that oppress and harm everyone, including those who created those systems in the first place. The Buddha was often called a "recluse" in his lifetime, with the proclamation that "Craving has been called an arrow by the Recluse." The Buddha is a prime example of someone who has walked away from the creation of those oppressive social and political systems.

Although the recorded teachings of the Buddha do not directly touch upon the oppressive social and political systems of his time, his life seems a potent reminder of how those environments can easily cause enormous damage through unleashing the arrows of craving and ignorance. It seems to me that the Buddha's way out of ignorance into liberation is as much

108 • Older and Wiser

a personal enterprise as it is a social and political commentary on human affairs.

That said, the ultimate issue is craving, not the systems. It is you and I who turn our craving into systems that come back to harm us and others.

The instructions of the Buddha with regard to a watchful stance toward craving and ignorance are a fair warning in our own processes of self-healing and healing the wounds of the world. We cannot hope to heal the wounds of the world without healing our own wounds embedded in craving and clinging. The spiral of craving can keep going upward forever, while the spiral of self-healing can keep going downward until the ending of craving gives way to the peace of *nibbāna*.

Reflections: Gloria Taraniya Ambrosia

There's a lot going on in this excerpt from the *Sunakkhatta Sutta*. Through the skillful use of simile, the Buddha outlines the progression from ignorance to liberation. Those of us who are intent on liberating the mind follow a prescribed path. Knowing we are beset by craving and ignorance, and supported by friends and companions, we give ourselves over to be guided by the skillful hands of the Buddha. He encourages us to practice sense restraint in order to offset attachment to the body and mind. Through mindfulness and wisdom, we take great care in our practice—that is, we do what is supportive of our purpose of uprooting the fetters, until we are certain that there is no trace left behind. In so doing, we offset the possibility of what the sutta calls "death and deadly suffering." Or, to put it in the vernacular, we do not regress on our path, revert to the old ways, or commit the kind of offenses that cause us to lose the support of our skillful companions or betray our confidence in the Buddha. Then, and only then, will we experience the fullness of non-attachment, *nibbāna*.

Admittedly, we seem to have to go through the painful surgical process of extracting the arrow and the surrounding poison. This is a process whereby we see for ourselves what it is like to linger in the poisonous, superficial layers of the mind where ignorance and craving dwell—ricocheting back and forth between likes and dislikes, desires and aversions, past and future. We also see for ourselves what it is like to be free of the arrow and surrounding poison. The awakening mind does the rest. We are hardwired to be able to sort this out.

Aging can be a huge support in this process. As we age, we quite naturally lose interest in worldly, material things. We discover that letting go … letting things be … brings the greatest happiness. My Dhamma buddy and I were talking just last week about what we call our increasing "world-weariness." Sensory objects simply don't have the pull they used to have—in part because we're too tired to keep grabbing them, but also because we have been garnering wisdom through years of practice. We are increasingly aware of the consequences of being caught in the endless quest for gratification. (We've seen it SO much … and it's exhausting!) Ironically, as we drop the quest, we discover that there is plenty of pleasure and happiness to go around. It's just the pain of the quest and the foolishness that we release. As time goes by, our new way of being in the world becomes rooted in our psyches. We are less and less likely to revert to the old ways. Yes, in the process of waking up we still get caught in craving and ignorance … that's unavoidable. But with mindfulness and patience we slowly clean the wound.

So perhaps the take-away from this sutta is this: Where are we in our practice? Do we see the extent of our craving for gratification? Are we aware of the ignorance that drives it? How deliberately are we using the probe of mindfulness to uproot craving and ignorance? How intent are we on *nibbāna*?

110 • Older and Wiser

4.4 Patient and Caregiver

Endowed with five qualities, one who is ill is easy to tend:

- one does what is beneficial;
- one knows moderation in what is beneficial;
- one takes medicine;
- one makes clear the disease just as it comes to be to one who tends the sick and who wishes him well, saying
  - as it is getting worse, 'It is getting worse,'
  - or as it is getting better, 'It is getting better,'
  - or as it is stable 'It is stable;'
- one becomes the kind of person who endures arising bodily feelings which are painful, acute, sharp, shooting, disagreeable, miserable, deadly.

Endowed with five qualities, one who tends the sick is fit to tend the sick:

- one is competent to provide the medicine;
- one knows what is beneficial and what is not beneficial;
- one takes away what is not beneficial, and brings forward what is beneficial;
- one tends the sick with a loving mind (*mettā-citta*), not in the hope of gain;
- one does not loathe to remove excrement or urine or sweat or vomit;
- one is competent to gladden, rejoice, rouse, and delight the sick from time to time with dhamma-talk.

(Mahāvagga 8:26)

Reflections: Andrew Olendzki

One of the most important components of the Buddha's teaching is the concept of interdependence, wherein things come to be how they are as a consequence of the interrelationship of multiple causes and conditions. This insight can be seen to work in most subtle ways when applied to understanding the interdependent arising of the mind and body and the nuanced teaching of non-self.

The idea of interdependence is also applied in many ways to the realm of human relationships, recognizing that all interactions are reciprocal. How one treats another person has much to do with how that person will treat you in return. When offering kindness, kindness is evoked from the other; when offering hostility, one is inviting and encouraging hostility in return. We can't help but recognize a form of the golden rule here—a universal truth recognized by all traditions.

In this text, the Buddha is approaching the matter of illness interdependently, identifying a reciprocal relationship between the patient and the caregiver. These two are actually partners in a shared enterprise, which unfolds optimally when each fulfills their role with integrity and thus enables the other to do their part effectively. We are used to focusing on the qualities of the caregiver, and indeed many professionals are well trained in how to provide skillful care. We are less familiar with the approach taken here, which emphasizes the equal importance of being a skillful patient.

Many times a patient is in such distress that the last thing one wants to do is place upon them any additional burden, such as expecting them to behave well as a patient. One certainly does not want to blame them for incontinence, for example, or get annoyed that they are in pain or chastise them for not healing faster, thus piling shame and guilt upon an already difficult situation. On the other hand, there may also be situations in which it is appropriate to have expectations of the patient, to encourage them to do their part and contribute to the partnership of healing. At the least, perhaps those of us who look to the *dhamma* for guidance can make a resolution that if (or when!) we find ourselves in this situation, we will do our best to be a good patient.

Much of what is said in the passage is obvious and is the product of good common sense (although I must say it is rather well put). More unusual is the last point regarding the patient, the recognition that at times one just has to accept that one will undergo experiences that are painful and difficult (even in an era of good drugs). Pain is amplified by resistance, thereby manifesting as suffering. Suffering is reduced if the aversion to pain can be diminished, and accepting "this is the way things are just now" can be a powerful tool for enduring difficult situations with the equanimity of mindfulness.

What is most striking about the last paragraph is the emphasis upon a loving cast of mind, as well as the ameliorative effects of hearing *dhamma* instruction as part of the healing process. The *dhamma* was taught by the Buddha "out of compassion for the welfare of beings" and will always be a friend to the afflicted.

Reflections: Mu Soeng

It seems to me that this text is a training manual in self-compassion for a person in the grip of aging, sickness, or dying processes. It teaches how to be patient with these processes, as well as how to be an ideal patient in the circumstances. The key phrase here is "in the circumstances." Our practice is how to be an ideal person, a noble person, a striver toward liberation in the circumstances of a happy and healthy life. A significant part of our practice is also to know that circumstances will change, and that the qualities we cultivate today in happy and healthy living will surely come in handy when we are in the grip of aging, sickness, and dying. After all, our training is to deal with whatever is arising (and passing away).

In this sense, an ideal patient is someone who trains oneself not to be a burden on others. An ideal patient would try to minimize the burden on the part of the nurse, most of all the compulsive need, seen in most human beings, to co-opt the nurse into the role of a fellow-sufferer. In other words, these are transference issues, and an untrained patient can very easily deceive himself or herself into believing that the nurse sees the world of pain and suffering in exactly the same way as the one who suffers. An ideal patient makes use of his/her training in practice to not impose anything extraneous on the nurse. It is almost a universal norm in medical care that a nurse will give greater care and attention to a patient who does not make unnecessary demands or impositions on the nurse. Therefore, an ideal patient is someone who has trained oneself in a certain degree of self-restraint.

The quality of self-restraint also appears in the first lines, "one knows moderation in what is beneficial," which reminds me of the vitamin craze from the early 1980s, when people were overdosing on vitamins on the assumption that "more is better." If two tabs of multivitamin a day is good for you, wouldn't twenty tabs a day benefit you ten times more? But that's the power of greed: we not only want to be healthy, we want to be super-healthy. Most people today know that overdosing on "good medicine" is the road to a lot of bad consequences.

When we practice moderation, we do so with the knowledge that in the world of radical impermanence, we can't hold on to anything at all, least of all our ideas of what it means to be healthy. A well-trained practitioner segues organically into an ideal patient when the time comes, where he or she practices compassion not only for oneself, but also for the nurse. The ideal nurse brings the same amount of caring and compassion to the act of nursing, knowing full well that in the great embrace of sickness and death the nurse will someday also be a patient.

Reflections: Gloria Taraniya Ambrosia

Many of the suttas in the Pāli Canon contain pithy and practical advice while also fostering skillful qualities of heart. The above sutta is a good example. Here the Buddha looks at both the patient and the caregiver with an eye to identifying qualities in each that will optimize their relationship and promote both physical and emotional well-being. This is a very timely reflection for us, as it is likely that in our senior years we will either be called upon to tend to a loved one who is sick or be in need of attendance ourselves.

As with our efforts to live by the precepts, we can try to embody the qualities outlined here by making a determination to follow them in a prescriptive way. That would be good enough. But we can take it a step further—ensuring that these qualities will be available to us when we need them—by working now to garner the insights out of which they naturally flow. Said another way ... how we respond in circumstances of sickness, aging, and death is predicated upon our level of insight into *anicca, dukkha,* and *anattā,* as well as our ability to act in accordance with what we have come to know and understand through our daily practice.

As we grow in our understanding of *anicca,* we are more at peace in the moment because we know that conditions are following natural laws, arising and passing according to their nature. Whether patient or caregiver, we are less likely to get ahead of ourselves. Thus, we can more easily focus on doing what is beneficial in the moment—addressing conditions carefully and without reactivity, complaints, or demands. With insight into *anicca,* there is greater presence of mind and greater presence of heart.

As we grow in our understanding of *dukkha,* we are more fortified in painful moments and thus less likely to get entangled with difficulty or lash out with aversion. Insight into the first noble truth lies at the heart of our capacity to bear difficult conditions. It carries with it the great paradox that when we understand suffering, we are more at peace with the way things are ... even happier. As a patient, "one becomes the kind of person who endures arising bodily feelings which are painful, etc." As a caregiver, one is not loathe to perform the unpleasant tasks at hand.

As we grow in our understanding of *anattā,* we are naturally less likely to quarrel with conditions over which we have no control. There is much less attachment to the body and mind, so one is able to view and even experience difficult conditions less personally. Insight into *anattā* forms the primary basis for letting go. When there is no quarrel, no battle with conditions ... there is the automatic arising of compassion. Wisdom and compassion are two sides of the same coin. With wisdom and compassion as our basis for action, attending to those who are sick, old, or dying is not a problem. Nor is enduring those conditions ourselves.

5. Death and Dying

5.1 The Divine Messengers

The story is told of a man who, having misbehaved during his lifetime, finds himself reborn in hell and standing before Yama, the god of death. King Yama questions, interrogates, and cross-examines him as follows: "Good man, did you not see the three divine messenger that appeared among human beings?" And the man replies, "No, lord, I did not see them."

Then King Yama says to him: "But, good man, did you not ever see among human beings:

- a man or a woman, eighty, ninety, or a hundred years of age, frail, bent like a roof bracket, crooked, wobbling as they go along leaning on a stick, ailing, youth gone, with broken teeth, with gray and scanty hair or bald, with wrinkled skin and blotched limbs? or,

- a man or a woman, sick, afflicted, gravely ill, lying in his own urine and excrement, having to be lifted up by some and put down by others? or,

- a man or a woman, one, two, or three days dead, the corpse bloated, livid, and festering?"

And the man replies: "Yes, lord, I have seen this."

Then King Yama says to him: "Good man, did it not occur to you, an intelligent and mature person: 'I too am subject to old age, illness, and death, I am not exempt from old age, illness and death. Let me now do good by body, speech, and mind'?"

"No, lord, I could not. I was heedless."

Then King Yama says: "Through heedlessness, good man, you failed to do good by body, speech, or mind. Surely, they will treat you in a way that fits your heedlessness. That bad kamma of yours was not done by your mother or father, nor by your brother or sister, nor by your friends and companions, nor by your relatives and family members, nor by the deities, nor by ascetics and brahmins. Rather, you were the one who did that bad kamma, and you yourself will have to experience its result."

The youths who remain neglectful,
Though warned by divine messengers,
Lament for a very long time:
They are bound for lower places.

But there are also people who,
When warned by divine messengers,
Do not neglect the noble way
At any time while they are here.

Seeing with dread that grasping is
The origin of birth and death,
They are released by not grasping,
And bring an end to birth and death.

They've reached safety and are happy,
Having here and now become quenched.
All fear and hate are left behind;
They've overcome all suffering.

(Anguttara Nikāya 3:35)

Reflections: Andrew Olendzki

I don't take seriously the legend that the Buddha as a young prince was so thoroughly protected from life that he had no exposure to aging, illness, or death until the age of twenty-nine. It seems more likely the episode of his riding through town with his charioteer and encountering these three signs (plus a fourth—the wandering ascetic) was attached to his biography in a dramatized form, having been adapted from this and similar passages in the early texts.

I also don't take too seriously this text's allusion to the punishments in the hell realms that await those who misbehave during life—this, too, I think is just a literary device for making the more poignant point that the evidence of our own mortality lies everywhere before our eyes. In the Buddha's teaching, of course, this is not meant to frighten or shame us, but rather to encourage us to make the best possible use of this precious human life. It is a call to heedfulness (*appamāda*), to paying careful attention to each moment of experience and to the quality of every deed, every word, and even every thought.

Notice what the realization of life slipping away immediately leads to in this text: a resolve to do good. Ask most people what is the appropriate response to the reality of diminishing days, and you are more likely to hear something like "getting the most out life," "doing all the things I want to do before I run out of time," or "accomplishing some great feat in order to leave a legacy." Instead, the emphasis here is upon improving one's character, having a beneficial effect on others, and living each moment with as much wholesomeness as possible.

Interestingly enough, these two ideals are not really at odds with each other. Those who practice mindfulness meditation know that it is in moments of maximum awareness that one gets the most out of life. Certainly, if I knew I had only moments to live, I would want each of those moments to be experienced as fully and with as much conscious awareness as possible. This is what the Buddha is pointing us toward with the image of living as if you were carrying a full vessel of oil on your head, followed by a swordsman with orders to lop off your head the moment a drop is spilled. A harsh image, to be sure, but again the point is in the quality of attention brought to each and every moment. A meditator might also realize that wanting to be the best person one can is the most noble thing to which one can aspire, and that cleansing the mind of toxins is indeed a great feat that leaves an inspiring legacy.

As life slips away, there is less to become attached to. Safety is within reach, by letting go of fear. Happiness is within reach, by releasing all hatred. And if this poem is to be believed, suffering can be overcome by allowing ourselves, here and now, to become quenched.

Reflections: Mu Soeng

The lines in the poem that those who have been warned by the divine messengers "do not neglect the noble way at any time while they are here," seem to point to the core of what I like to call the "Buddhist civilization." My own provisional definition of Buddhist civilization is that it is a culture or civilization of restraint and renunciation. It also seems to me that what we call "mindfulness" is more about paying heed to this "warning" of the divine messengers. When we put it all together, the "noble way" of the Buddha is to be mindful of the hazards the mind-body will inevitably go through in the processes of aging and sickness.

The "noble way" of the Buddha (though many will continue to subscribe to the idea of eat, drink, and be merry) is a template for crafting our way in the world without losing sight of the "divine messengers" hovering always in the background. This awareness, rather than being debilitating, has been an impetus in traditional religious and shamanic cultures to diligently attend to one's chosen path.

For a Buddhist practitioner, diligently cultivating the eightfold path nestles itself within the framework of *dukkha*, which is none other than the message of the divine messengers. The cultivation of the eightfold path is the cultivation of a personal and societal culture of restraint and renunciation. Of course, this is all counterintuitive and countercultural. One cannot expect support for this point of view from those near and dear. The eightfold path and its worldview therefore becomes a journey of aloneness (without being lonely). The function of a community is to allow one to be "alone with others," in Stephen Batchelor's elegant phrase.

The message of the divine messengers and the journey of aloneness, which allows one to listen carefully to that message, is a positive inspiration. Aging and sickness are not metaphysical speculations, nor is the path of their acceptance with equanimity and grace. And, yes, equanimity and grace will come only through letting go of all clinging and fear. And that letting go will come through wholesome view, wholesome intention, wholesome mindfulness, and so on.

I find it interesting, within the historical Buddhist tradition, that a very large percentage of Buddha's early disciples joined the sangha at a young age (either in their teenage years or in their twenties), which leads me to believe that they heard the message of the divine messengers loud and clear. Our challenge today is how to craft our own lives in order to be able to hear that message.

Reflections: Gloria Taraniya Ambrosia

We probably all know people who don't want to think about, talk about, or consider the realities of aging, sickness, and death. If we attempt to engage them in a conversation about these facts of life, they might even think we are macabre or depressed. However, the Buddha encouraged us to let these realities into our hearts. "THERE IS aging, sickness, and death," he said. Birth includes these inevitable conditions. This, he says, must be understood.

You'd think we would know this ... but like the culprit in the above sutta, we may be only vaguely aware ... only vaguely opening to these realities. Thus, we don't have the necessary data or the insight to optimize this human birth, to relate to one another with kindness, compassion, and skill, and to free our hearts from delusion. As the sutta suggests, ignorance has consequences. One remains bound to *samsāra,* bound to suffering.

But while some people ignore the truth, there are those who "do not neglect the noble way." They open to the realities of our human condition and thereby overcome the craving at the root of ignorance. In other words, by understanding the first noble truth, we overcome the second noble truth (the cause of suffering), and realize the third noble truth (cessation). For those who realize the noble truths, there is no more birth and death.

So the whole process of awakening is predicated on understanding that there is suffering ... which includes awakening to the realities of aging, sickness, and death. Admittedly, opening in this way tends to be a slow process. As practitioners, we begin to see the delusion that obstructs clear seeing; we see our resistance to conditions as they are and the longing for things to be different. If we're honest, most of us will admit that we expend a tremendous amount of energy trying to ward off aging, sickness, and death. It's rare indeed for anyone to embrace these without a struggle. It may be a rude awakening, but for all our efforts we haven't realized eternal youth. We haven't overcome sickness in any ultimate way. And we haven't figured out how to cheat the grim reaper. Nobody gets out alive. We're going to die ... it's just a matter of when, where, and whether we can do it with grace.

But it's not all bad news. As the verses at the end of the sutta suggest, there's a great paradox here. As we wake up to these seemingly grim realities, we find we are much happier because our conditioned response of longing, resistance, and ignoring diminishes. "Wow! Life includes aging, sickness, and death ... and I'm actually okay." The divine messengers are the doorways to freedom. We wake up to the first noble truth, and we wake up to life. We embrace life on its terms. The process may not be fun, but afterwards we are better for it. We relax into the reality of our existence. Our suffering is not in these conditions themselves but in our inability to see their reality and accept it.

124 • Older and Wiser

5.2 Learning to Let Go

On one occasion the householder Anāthapiṇḍika was afflicted, suffering, and gravely ill.
The venerable Sāriputta dressed and, taking his bowl and outer robe, went to the residence of Anāthapiṇḍika with Ānanda as his attendant.
Having gone there, he sat down on a seat made ready and said to Anāthapiṇḍika:

"I hope you are getting well, I hope you are comfortable.
I hope your painful feelings are subsiding and not increasing."

"Venerable Sāriputta, I am not getting well, I am not comfortable.
My painful feelings are increasing, not subsiding.

> Just as if a strong man were splitting my head open with a sharp sword,
> so too, violent winds cut through my head.

> Just as if a strong man were tightening a tough leather strap around my head as a headband,
> so too, there are violent pains in my head.

> Just as if a skilled butcher or his apprentice
> were to carve up an ox's belly with a sharp butcher's knife,
> so too, violent winds are carving up my belly.

> Just as if two strong men were to seize a weaker man
> by both arms and roast him over a pit of hot coals,
> so too, there is a violent burning in my body."

Then, householder, said Sāriputta, you should train thus:

> "I will not cling to the eye, ear, nose, tongue, body, or mind, and my consciousness will not be dependent on these.

> I will not cling to forms, sounds, smells, tastes, touches, or mind-objects,

> and my consciousness will not be dependent on these.

Death and Dying • 125

I will not cling to seeing, hearing, smelling, tasting, touching or thinking,
and my consciousness will not be dependent on these.

I will not cling to eye-contact, ear-contact, nose-contact, tongue-contact, body-contact, or mind-contact,
and my consciousness will not be dependent on these.

I will not cling to feeling born of eye-contact, feeling born of ear-contact, feeling born of nose-contact, feeling born of tongue-contact, feeling born of body-contact, feeling born of mind-contact,
and my consciousness will not be dependent on these.

I will not cling to the earth element, the water element, the fire element, the air element,
and my consciousness will not be dependent on these.

I will not cling to material form, feeling, perception, formations, consciousness,
and my consciousness will not be dependent on these.

I will not cling to this world or the world beyond,
and my consciousness will not be dependent on these.

I will not cling to what is seen, heard, sensed, cognized, encountered, sought after and examined by the mind,
and my consciousness will not be dependent on these.

When this was said, Anāthapiṇḍika wept and shed tears, saying,

Although I have long waited upon the Teacher and bhikkhus worthy of esteem, never before have I heard such a talk on the Dhamma.
Let such talk on the Dhamma be given to lay people clothed in white.
There are people with little dust in their eyes who are wasting away through not hearing such talk on the Dhamma.
There will be those who will understand."

Then, after giving Anāthapinkika this advice,
Sāriputta and Ānanda rose from their seats and departed.

126 • Older and Wiser

Soon after they had left, the householder Anāthapinkika died.

(*Anāthapiṇḍika Sutta, Majjhima Nikāya 143*)

Reflections: Andrew Olendzki

This is a poignant scene, for clearly Anāthapiṇḍika, who was one of the Buddha's earliest and most important lay supporters, is on his deathbed. Sāriputta is offering him release from his afflictions, but not in the ways we might expect. After the initial formal exchange of asking after his health (in a standard formula found in many other texts), he goes on to help Anāthapiṇḍika free his mind from its entanglements with life, and thus ease his passing away rather than trying to impede it by denial or the uttering of platitudes.

I believe this text is intended as a guided meditation, and as such it is meant to be gone through slowly and experientially. I have condensed it significantly from its original form, in which each of the fifty-two items listed gets individual attention. Sāriputta is leading Anāthapiṇḍika through the landscape of inner experience, through the phenomenal field of his lived experience, and inviting him at each step to let go, to release the subtle clinging that binds us to life, and to thus release his consciousness from the attachments that constitute suffering. Perhaps this is the greatest gift one can give to the dying.

The stories Anāthapiṇḍika attaches to his afflictions, of strong men seizing and afflicting him, only serve to amplify the physical distress with which he must inevitably cope. As with the teaching of two arrows (See 4.2: *Stabbed by One Arrow— Not Two*), it is an unnecessary and unhelpful conceptual overlay to the situation. Instead, Sāriputta escorts him into the phenomenological details of his senses, and invites the gentle relaxation of his mind's grasping fingers upon all it directly encounters. This particular unpleasant sensation arising with this specific sensory input? Let go of that. And this particular emotional response to this specific arising thought-moment?

Let that go, too. Let it all go, for there is nothing you have to hold on to anymore.

My father abided bravely with the rapid advance of the cancer that arose unexpectedly in his esophagus. He was clearly doing it for my sister and I, eating when we told him to and taking the pills we put before him. But at the very end, in one of those very lucid moments, I looked into his eyes and told him gently that he did not have to hold on anymore. He looked at me with surprise at first, then with understanding, and finally with what I can only recall as a sense of relief and even the hint of a smile. He was gone within the hour, and it was a peaceful end.

We need not wait until our final moments to practice this deep unhanding of our experience. Touch everything, but cling to nothing. Consciousness can be aware of things without becoming dependent upon them. As the meditation instructions in the *Satipaṭṭhāna Sutta* put it, consciousness can be free in this very life when we learn to "abide without clinging to anything whatsoever in this world."

Reflections: Mu Soeng

The backdrop of this story should be familiar to most of us. We all have been in situations where a friend in older years is narrating the difficulties he or she is having. Most of the time we respond by offering platitudes about life being difficult, but we are not always sure what is being asked of us.

This story turns our habitual ways of doing things upside down. Remember, Anāthapiṇḍika and Sāriputta are both senior disciples of the Buddha and have known each other for a very long time (Anāthapiṇḍika was the wealthy merchant who was an early and generous supporter of the Buddha and his monks; Sāriputta was the foremost among all disciples in cultivation of wisdom), but here Anāthapiṇḍika is falling into the trap of losing his equanimity to the pains in the body.

It is a common enough human experience that sickness often triggers great physical pain, especially when one is in older years.

128 • Older and Wiser

In fact, for some people (Woody Allen comes to mind), dying would be all right if it wasn't so damn painful! The concurrence of aging and dying resulting in physical pain is amply evoked by Anāthapiṇḍika when he describes his symptoms to his old friend Sāriputta.

Sāriputta's response is unwavering even in the face of his old friend's difficult situation. He is completely honest in asserting that the aversion displayed by Anāthapiṇḍika in his dying processes is really no different from aversion (or greed) while one is young and in good health. The antidote to greed and aversion, whether one is young or old, healthy or sick, is the same: do not cling to whatever is arising in the domain of the sense-fields.

It may seem to some that Sāriputta is being unkind in not humoring his friend's complaints about his body pains, but on closer examination we may see great compassion in Sāriputta's response. Tradition tells us that Anāthapiṇḍika became a stream-enterer as a result of his listening to Buddha's teachings over many years. As such, he is not expected to fall prey to these paralyzing thoughts. Even though Sāriputta's response is a fairly standard and somewhat formulaic Buddhist teaching, he seems to be implicitly reminding Anāthapiṇḍika of his meditative and wisdom accomplishments of the past. In other words, he is saying, "Old friend, don't backslide now." This is a sign of deep friendship—of a true *kalyāna-mitta*.

Anāthapiṇḍika sheds tears of gratitude at being reminded of all that he has heard from the Buddha over the years and put into practice. I would like to hope that all of us can have a *kalyāna-mitta* like Sāriputta who will not offer vacuous platitudes during the difficult transition into sickness, aging, and dying, but will remind us, honestly, that clinging is the root cause of our suffering. If we can't let go of clinging when the moment of death is imminent, what is the point of practice?

Indeed, the practice of not-clinging while we are well and healthy creates a habit-groove that can be reclaimed in the difficult moments of aging and dying. Anāthapiṇḍika seems distracted enough to lose sight of that habit-groove, and Sāriputta, like a true friend, is simply reminding him of it.

Reflections: Gloria Taraniya Ambrosia

We may feel a debt of gratitude to Anāthapiṇḍika for requesting this teaching. Such practice-specific teachings were not taught to the laity before the time of Anāthapiṇḍika's request and, had he not encouraged Venerable Sāriputta to offer this teaching to the laity, who knows if it would have remained only within the purview of ascetic practitioners.

This is an intense scene. One can feel Anāthapiṇḍika's torment. The graphic description of his violent and burning pain seems to jump off the page. We know from the suttas that on two previous occasions Anāthapiṇḍika had requested that a monk visit his sickbed. On the first occasion, Venerable Ānanda came; on the second, Venerable Sāriputta came. Both times, Anāthapiṇḍika recovered from his illness—one time seemingly miraculously. But this time was different. There is evidence from the full sutta that Venerable Sāriputta knew death was imminent. As if to demonstrate that circumstances were dire, this time both monks called upon Anāthapiṇḍika.

I find it interesting that Venerable Sāriputta did not try to soften the blow of Anāthapiṇḍika's illness or deflect his attention by offering superficial promises of relief. Instead, he gave a teaching that implicitly acknowledged the conditions of our lives ... but encouraging a new way of relating. He addressed the profound suffering of attachment, the suspension of which promised the only true relief. In so doing, Venerable Sāriputta offered one of the most comprehensive teachings on non-attachment, the ultimate guide to release. Venerable Sāriputta instructed Anāthapiṇḍika to free himself from clinging to the six sense bases and their objects and to the consciousness associated with these ... to free himself from clinging to the connecting link between the six sense bases and their objects, as well as to the six sense contacts, the six feelings, the four elements, the five aggregates, the four formless realms, and all that is seen, heard, thought, perceived, and investigated in the mind.

We know from other suttas that Anāthapiṇḍika was a stream-enterer. As such, we can surmise that he already knew about attachment to the body and mind, as well as the suffering associated with clinging to the five aggregates as self … and all the rest of it. But there is a big difference between insight into these truths and our capacity to consistently bring that understanding to bear on the moment. Now, with his back against the wall, he must have been practicing with non-attachment as he had never practiced before. For no sooner had Venerable Sāriputta finished his teaching, then it became clear that Anāthapiṇdika was experiencing great relief.

Like Anāthapiṇdika, we all have heard this kind of teaching before. Most of us have practiced diligently with it much of our adult lives. As a result, I'm sure that we are carrying a lighter load. But this sutta challenges us to apply ourselves to the direct experience of non-attachment with renewed enthusiasm … to practice with the urgency that Anāthapiṇdika must have felt … that is, as if we were at death's door. How will we respond to Venerable Sāriputta's no-nonsense guidance? It is our turn to practice like we have never practiced before!

5.3 Taking One's Life

On one occasion, the Buddha was dwelling at Rājagaha in the Bamboo Grove, the Squirrel Sanctuary.

Now on that occasion the Venerable Vakkali was dwelling in a potter's shed, sick, afflicted, gravely ill.

Then Vakkali addressed his attendants: "Come, friends, approach the Buddha, pay homage to him in my name with your head at his feet, and say: 'Venerable sir, the bhikkhu Vakkali is sick, afflicted, gravely ill; he pays homage to the Buddha with his head at his feet.' Then say: 'It would be good, venerable sir, if the Buddha would approach the bhikkhu Vakkali out of compassion.'"

"Yes, friend," those bhikkhus replied, and they approached the Buddha, paid homage to him, sat down to one side, and delivered their message. The Buddha consented by silence.

Then the Buddha dressed and, taking bowl and robe, approached the bhikkhu Vakkali. Vakkali saw the Buddha coming in the distance and stirred on his bed. The Buddha said to him: "Enough, Vakkali, do not stir on your bed. There are these seats ready, I will sit down there."

The Buddha then sat down on the appointed seat and said to Vakkali: "I hope you are bearing up, Vakkali, I hope you are getting better. I hope that your painful feelings are subsiding and not increasing, and that their subsiding, not their increase, is to be discerned."

"Venerable sir, I am not bearing up, I am not getting better. Strong painful feelings are increasing in me, not subsiding, and their increase, not their subsiding, is to be discerned."

"I hope then, Vakkali, that you are not troubled by remorse and regret."

"Indeed, venerable sir, I have quite a lot of remorse and regret."

"I hope, Vakkali, that you have nothing for which to reproach yourself in regard to virtue."

"I have nothing, venerable sir, for which to reproach myself in regard to virtue."

"Then, Vakkali, if you have nothing for which to reproach yourself in regard to virtue, why are you troubled by remorse and regret?"

"For a long time, venerable sir, I have wanted to come to see the Buddha, but I haven't been fit enough to do so."

"Enough, Vakkali! Why do you want to see this foul body? One who sees the Dhamma sees me; one who sees me sees the Dhamma. For in seeing the Dhamma, Vakkali, one sees me; and in seeing me, one sees the Dhamma."

Then the Buddha, having given [an] exhortation to Vakkali [regarding the aggregates and their impermanence], rose from his seat and departed for Vulture Peak.

Then, when the night had passed, the Buddha addressed the bhikkhus thus: "Come, bhikkhus, approach the bhikkhu Vakkali and say to him: 'Friend Vakkali, do not be afraid! Your death will not be a bad one. Your demise will not be a bad one.'"

"Yes, venerable sir," those bhikkhus replied, and they approached Vakkali ... [and related what the Buddha said. Vakkhali replied:]

"Well then, friends, pay homage to the Buddha in my name with your head at his feet and say: 'Venerable sir, the bhikkhu Vakkali is sick, afflicted, gravely ill; he pays homage to the Buddha with his head at his feet.' Then say:

- 'Form is impermanent ...
- Feeling is impermanent ...
- Perception is impermanent ...
- Volitional formations are impermanent ...
- Consciousness is impermanent: I have no perplexity about this, venerable sir. I do not doubt that whatever

is impermanent is suffering. I do not doubt that in regard to what is impermanent, suffering, and subject to change, I have no more desire, lust, or affection.'"

"Yes, friend," those bhikkhus replied, and then they departed.

Then, not long after those bhikkhus had left, the Venerable Vakkali used the knife.

(Samyutta Nikāya 22:87)

Reflections: Andrew Olendzki

When we focus attention on matters relating to aging, illness, and death, it is inevitable that the issue of taking one's own life will eventually emerge. The Buddhist texts seem ambiguous on this point. On the one hand it is not condoned, and is even discouraged, but there are other stories in which it seems to be tolerated and not particularly condemned. As with everything else in Buddhist ethics, I think it ultimately has less to do with the outcome and more to do with one's intention or state of mind at the moment of initiating the action.

Suicide that is driven by despair and an intense longing to escape the current conditions of life cannot be a healthy thing. Nor can it be healthy to be craving a better existence in the future, for such an action to be motivated by a longing for a better rebirth. Each of these choices is rooted in aversion and attachment, respectively. The midpoint between these two emotions is equanimity, an evenly-balanced state of being mindful and aware but not inclining toward or away from anything in particular. Is it possible to take one's own life in a state of equanimity? One can imagine a scenario in which one takes a level-headed look at what lies ahead, the prospects for recovery, for pain, for disruption to loved ones or to finances or to one's dignity—and decide, as Vakkali did, to "use the knife."

What I find more interesting in this exchange is the Buddha's response to Vakkali's impending death. He asks if there is anything for which Vakkali has remorse and regret, and if there

134 • Older and Wiser

is any past conduct for which Vakkali might reproach himself. It seems that dying with a clear conscience is important, and this is why a life lived ethically is such a gift to oneself in the final moments of life. If there are grounds for reproach, it makes sense to unburden oneself of such things before facing death. This is where asking and granting forgiveness might make a big difference, and in Buddhist countries there are formal ways of doing this. Karma is a system of storing causes and effects and paying them forward, so the more one can do to clear one's accounts, the better off one will be. Regardless of what really happens when we die (and who really knows?), the point here is entering into the experience with an open and unburdened mind, without guilt or shame, and therefore without fear.

Also interesting in the passage is that the Buddha chooses to talk to Vakkali about the impermanence of the aggregates and the importance of detaching oneself from grasping after them (much as he did with Anāthapiṇḍika in the previous teaching (See 5.2: *Learning to Let Go*). Vakkali's final message to the Buddha is that he has indeed reached the point of understanding the nature of his experience to the extent that he can disengage from the flow of phenomena and let it all slip away without grasping. When the Buddha receives this message, he declares to the assembled monks that Vakkali was an arahant. Interesting that even an arahant can use the knife and take his own life.

Reflections: Mu Soeng

It would have been really nice to know if there was any follow-up dialogue, short-term or long-term, among the monks about the advisability of suicide under certain circumstances. Unfortunately, the Pāli Canon is organized only around the discourses of the Buddha or, in rare cases, senior disciples. So we are left to our own devices in sorting out this perplexing yet fundamental issue.

There are only a handful of references in the Pāli Canon to the issue of bhikkhu suicide. Among these cases are those of monks Godhika, Channa, and Vakkali, all of whom committed suicide because of debilitating physical pain. In each case, the Buddha does not take a definitive position on suicide but pronounces each one of them to be *parinibbutta*, or someone having attained *nibbāna*. In other words, they had the consciousness of an arahant in their dying moment.

It does not follow from these examples that every bhikkhu who ever committed suicide was an arahant. But these examples do provoke us to ask what the issue is and what's at stake here? Is suicide a moral issue? What makes it (or anything else) a moral issue? One definition of morality is that an act is desirable and beneficial for the largest number of people. But "desirable" and "beneficial" can be slippery slopes and may depend on who is doing the defining. In any case, the taking of others' lives is not a desirable thing. It is an absolute prohibition in Buddha's teaching.

What about taking another's life indirectly? This takes us into the issue of eating meat, which seems to sanction an indirect killing of life on one's behalf. What about taking one's own life under horrible circumstances? Who is to decide what circumstances are horrible enough to warrant this act?

Then we have the controversial example of Vietnamese monks burning themselves in public as a political protest. We have also seen Tibetan monks immolating themselves in public as a protest against the Chinese genocide of their culture and religion.

In this *sutta*, Venerable Vakkali seems to be saying that in his subjective experience his circumstances are horrible. In response, the Buddha seems to be implying that one's intentions need to be investigated very clearly. This seems to imply that the role of clear and wholesome intention in the subjectivity of making choices is supreme.

Can we interpret the supremacy of intention as a moral text? I think we are forced back to the basic wisdom template in the eightfold path of right view and right intention in exploring this issue. The exploration of "view" leads us to ask what gets defined as a "horrible" life circumstance and/or what is an appropriate view of any given life circumstance.

The exploration of "intention" leads us to consider what should be done when we categorize a specific life circumstance as desirable or undesirable, regardless of any other consideration. So the ending of one's physical pain as the absolute determinant in setting up an intention seems to be what Venerable Vakkali is advocating and, in my reading, the Buddha seems to be agreeing.

We should also take note that the language of "sanctity of life" (as it is often presented in Christian theology) is not part of Buddhist frameworks. Rather, the "taking of life" is fundamental to these frameworks. Again, the role of intention becomes necessarily central here. This was also one of the distinctions the Buddha made in his doctrinal debates with his contemporary Jain practitioners, who preached that an unintentional taking of life (such as unknowingly stepping on an ant or other insect) will have karmic consequences. As inheritors of Western intellectual and religious traditions, we have to wrestle with these frameworks with the knowledge that they can be deeply problematic in defining what is "moral" or what is "ethical."

At least one scholarly article on the issue of suicide in the Pāli Canon addresses it in the context of the society and culture of Buddha's time. That context may not be very helpful to us today, but suicide, under certain circumstances, remains a deeply human problem. It is an invitation for us to investigate it carefully in our own time and place. How can we explore the issue of intention and view in our practice, and how we calibrate that practice to our own issues of aging and dying?

Reflections: Gloria Taraniya Ambrosia

During one of our yearlong programs, while we were contemplating the five precepts, questions arose around suicide and the first precept. Interestingly, there seemed to be general agreement that suicide involved the taking of life, and therefore a transgression of the first precept. But there was also a prevailing feeling that it's probably not that simple.

The Buddhist teachings can help us consider the issue from several angles.

(1) Understanding the precepts

First, it's good to remember that the precepts are not mandates for behavior. Nor are they the Buddha's effort to pit what is right against what is wrong. Yes, they are training guidelines, so they seem to imply that there is a right and a wrong thing to do. But it's actually more correct to view them as pointers—to areas where we are easily tripped up and lose sight of our capacity to live a harmless life, or where we fail to fully align our actions through body, speech, and mind with our aspiration to be kind and compassionate ... and to wake up. We use the precepts as guidelines to help us move in the direction of right view and right intention.

When it comes to the first precept, it's not so much a question of whether or not suicide is wrong. It's more an invitation to consider the intention behind the act. Is it possible to take life without arousing or strengthening unskillful, unhealthy, or deluded states of mind?

This sutta seems to answer that question. Here we have a monk, Vakkali, who is an arahant. As such, we must conclude that his mind had been purified of greed, hatred, and delusion and that the act of suicide was completely motivated by compassion. This would seem to suggest that in the case of an arahant it is possible to commit suicide without incurring weighty karma—without transgressing the first precept. For the rest of us ... I would say it is a question of whether or not one's action proceeds from a level of compassion that at least approaches that of an arahant. Hmm. Lots to think about here.

(2) What constitutes release from suffering?

It is also helpful to remember that (in Buddhist practice) the suffering that we are trying to overcome is not measured in terms of physical pain or even mental torment, per se. Pain goes with the territory of having a body and mind, and our practice involves waking up to that fact. Yes, we want to ease physical and mental suffering when we see it, but ultimately the suffering we are trying to overcome is the suffering of craving and ignorance. Said another way ... it's not the physical or mental pain that is problematic. It's the delusion that causes us to want to live a painless life.

So as we wake up, our response to physical and mental pain changes—that is, we see that these do not need to be eradicated in order for us to find peace. Peace happens as we diminish the tendency to quarrel with conditions and as we open to and accept the fact that physical and mental suffering are a consequence of birth.

Contemplating in this way would seem to suggest that it's okay to commit suicide. There is no judgment here. However, ... barring certainty that, like Vakkali, one's intention is purified of greed, hatred, and delusion ... and given that, if not, the act might carry some weighty karma ... perhaps the question becomes: is it worth the gamble? In the end, we must decide for ourselves. Fortunately, for most of us, this is not a question that we will have to answer.

5.4 Facing Death Without Concern

On one occasion the Buddha was dwelling among the Bhaggas at Sumsumāragira, in the deer park at Bhesakalā Grove. Now on that occasion the householder Nakulapitā was sick, afflicted, gravely ill. Then the housewife Nakulamātā said this to him:

"Do not die full of concern. To die full of concern is painful.

> 1. "To die full of concern has been criticized by the Blessed One." It may be that you think thus: 'After I'm gone, Nakulamātā won't be able to support our children and maintain the household.' But you should not look at the matter in this way. I am skilled at weaving cotton and knitting wool. After you are gone, I'll be able to support the children and maintain the household.
>
> 2. "It may be that you think thus: 'After I'm gone, Nakulamātā will take another husband.' But you should not look at the matter in this way. You know, and so do I, that for the last sixteen years we have led the layperson's celibate life.
>
> 3. "It may be that you think thus: 'After I'm gone, Nakulamātā won't want to see the Blessed One and the Sangha of bhikkhus.' But you should not look at the matter in this way. After you are gone, I will be even keener to see the Buddha and the Sangha of bhikkhus.
>
> 4. "It may be that you think thus: 'After I'm gone, Nakulamātā will not fulfill virtuous behavior.' But you should not look at the matter in this way. I am one of the Buddha's white-robed female lay disciples who fulfill virtuous behavior.
>
> 5. "It may be that you think thus: 'After I'm gone, Nakulamātā will not obtain internal serenity of mind.' But you should not look at the matter in this way. I am one of

140 • Older and Wiser

the Buddha's white-robed female lay disciples who obtain internal serenity of mind.

6. "It may be that you think thus: 'Nakulamātā has not attained a foothold, a firm stand, assurance in this Dhamma and discipline; she has not crossed over doubt, gotten rid of bewilderment, attained self-confidence, and become independent of others in the Teacher's teaching.' But you should not look at the matter in this way. [I have done all this.]"

Then, while the householder Nakulapitā was being exhorted in this way by the housewife Nakulamātā, his ailment subsided on the spot. Nakulapitā recovered from that illness, and that is how his illness was abandoned.

Then, not long after he had recovered, the householder Nakulapitā, leaning on a staff, approached the Buddha. He paid homage to the Buddha and sat down to one side. The Buddha then said to him:

"It is truly your good fortune and gain, householder, that the housewife Nakulamātā has compassion for you, desires your good, and exhorts and instructs you."

(Anguttara Nikāya 6:16)

Reflections: Andrew Olendzki

In the further adventures of the intrepid lay Buddhist couple, Nakulapitā and Nakulamātā (Father and Mother Nakula), we share a poignant moment when Father appears to be on his deathbed. Mother, as always, is full of love and affection for her husband, and out of compassion encourages him to be at peace as he dies. The phrasing here seems harsh to our ears, that the Buddha "criticizes" being "full of concern," but this is more a matter of translation than of substance. The tone is one of understanding what is helpful and harmful and wanting what is best for Father, rather than rebuking him for somehow dying badly.

The issue here is that Father is very concerned for the well-being of his partner, and I suspect this is a common concern for many at this point of life. We want those we leave behind to be safe and well and happy, even while understanding that our own death will naturally cause much distress. Mother Nakula is not telling him that she will not suffer from his passing away, only that she is strong enough that the pain of losing him will not unbalance her entirely, and able enough to care for her own well-being in his absence. Practically (by her weaving), emotionally (by her non-interest in taking another husband), and spiritually (by her deep and unshakable commitment to the Buddha's teachings), she feels confident enough to reassure Father not to be unnecessarily distressed on her account.

As often happens in this kind of story, Father experiences a surprising recovery, and the whole matter is postponed for a time. The Buddha, showing a rare and touching human side, reminds Father Nakula of his good fortune in having such a caring wife. Notice that her virtues include not only having compassion for him and wishing his welfare, but also a willingness to "exhort and instruct" him. This is a theme found elsewhere in the texts as well, wherein it becomes a duty and responsibility of a good friend or companion to help keep a person on the straight path by admonishing them from time to time if necessary.

The heart of the matter, as always, is grasping or attachment. It always benefits us to unburden ourselves of the things we cling to, but this is especially important at the end of life. However we might construe what happens next, the Buddha is encouraging us to face it with a tranquil and peaceful mind. If this is the end, it is a fitting and dignified end; if it is the gateway to another life, then let us step through calmly and with an open mind; if it is the beginning of an extended term of bliss, we might as well set off on the right foot; and if things are about to get a good deal more difficult, let's relish the peace while we can.

There are not many gifts we can give a person who is about to pass away, but peace of mind may be a very precious one.

142 • Older and Wiser

Reflections: Mu Soeng

This text is quite interesting on multiple levels. Besides reflecting on the issue of facing the death of a loved one with equanimity, it establishes a chronology for a flourishing four-fold "sangha" during the lifetime of the Buddha: the *bhikkhus*, the *bhikkunis*, the *upāsakā* (male lay followers), and the *upāsikā* (female lay followers).

Both Nakulapitā and his wife are described as lay ordained followers. If their exchange is any indication, the bold statement by Nakulamātā that her dying husband should not doubt the stability of her practice of Dhamma and Vinaya (ethical discipline) is an indication of a self-assurance equal to any monk's. The further implication is that her dying husband, even though he has been on the same path for the same length of time, has not progressed as much as she has. He does not have confidence in his practice; his mind is still full of concern with trivial matters.

The Buddha, when apprised of the particulars of the situation, is appreciative of Nakulamātā's compassion and generosity in advancing her husband's understanding of the path. Nakulamātā says to her husband that [through her practice of *sīla*, *samādhi*, and *paññā*] she has obtained "internal serenity of mind."

This internal serenity of mind is what was needed for her to remain equanimous when it was clear that her husband was dying, as well as to remain equally equanimous when her own moment of death became imminent. The historical importance of this passage may be its acknowledgment that it is just as possible for lay people to obtain the internal serenity of mind as it is for monks.

The necessary corollary of the exchange between husband and wife is that the internal peace she has obtained requires a long, disciplined effort to train oneself, and she has put in the requisite effort. Another corollary is that through the internal peace she has obtained, she is dealing with "life" as it is unfolding for her in that moment, namely, a dying husband. The obvious conclusion is that since we will never know the precise moment of our own death, we are left with the ever-present moments of life in which the aging, sickness, and dying of those around us hold up a mirror for us to see our own ever-present moments of life—and to maintain the internal serenity of mind.

In this dharma understanding, there cannot be any "future" moment that may be called the "moment of death." All we have, and all we will ever have, are these moments of "life." We train in this moment, and we investigate this moment fully, and we develop internal serenity in this moment—not for the sake of some future moment, but to engage most fully with this moment. The reassurance of the Buddha is that a well-established internal serenity of mind will take care of all the moments that are yet to come.

If we do it with confidence, as Nakulamātā has done, the next moment will flow into this present moment's internal serenity and will find its natural resolution, regardless of whether it's a moment of death or life.

Reflections: Gloria Taraniya Ambrosia

Perhaps the primary message of this sutta is that we would all be wise to get a handle on "worry and flurry" while we are still in good health, lest it become a major hindrance when we are facing death. Suffering, which is an inescapable fact of life, is compounded by attaching to restless and agitated thinking. We need to overcome that … or at least learn how to maneuver around it.

This isn't easy to do. The unawakened mind is very much given to fabricating stories that feed upon and magnify feelings of fear and anxiety. Our task as meditators is to see this tendency and develop the necessary serenity of mind to meet it head on—to see anxious thinking without buying into it or hating it. Perhaps more than any work we might do in practice, this capacity will support an easeful death.

I've spoken with a number of people recently who have lost one or both of their parents. They all spoke of their parents' need to be reassured that everyone will be okay after they die. This is a common anxiety among all people … but particularly among parents. It is a subtle attachment that may be one of the ways in which we deflect our attention away from the dying process itself.

A week or two before my own mother died, she asked my sisters and I, brothers-in-law, nieces, and nephews to gather around her and "huddle together." She insisted that we sit close enough to be touching one another. She needed to know that we would care for one another after she was gone. And, indeed, this reassurance seemed to help her let go. At the time this was very touching and remains one of the sweetest memories of the days leading to her death, but when I contemplate the anxiety from which it may have proceeded, I feel sad for her. I have vowed to try to offset that kind of anxiety should it arise at the time of my own death. As Buddhist practitioners, we want to focus all of our attention on letting go. It's never too late to overcome grasping.

Nakulapitā's concerns distracted him, too. He wanted to be reassured that his wife would be able to support the family, and he couldn't relax until he was reassured that Nakulamātā would stay focused on her spiritual training. Ironically, this concern for his wife's spiritual practice was ill-placed. It is clear that Nakulamātā was a stream enterer … as evidenced by her stated confidence in the Dhamma and discipline. Because he himself had not realized the first stage of awakening, he could not see that his wife had done so. His energy might have been better spent focusing on his own practice!

It's a little puzzling (and possibly confusing) that "while being exhorted in this way" Nakulapitā was miraculously restored to health. Perhaps the Buddha wants us to contemplate the link between attachment to the hindrances and ill health. Or perhaps the message here is that serenity of mind is powerful medicine. I don't know. But without evidence that Nakulapitā had realized significant insight prior to becoming gravely ill, the fact that he overcame his illness upon hearing the teachings must be nothing more than a happy coincidence. I'm quite sure that the Buddha is not offering this story to promote magical thinking!

6. Mourning

6.1 Ānanda Alone

Just before the Buddha passed away, on the morning of his *parinibbāna*, Ānanda, his cousin and lifelong companion, slips away and stands weeping in the doorway of his lodging. The Buddha calls for him and addresses him with great poignancy and compassion:

> Enough, Ānanda.
> Do not weep; do not lament.
> Has this not already been shown
> by me to be so:
> All that is dear and charming
> becomes different,
> becomes naught,
> becomes other than it is?
>
> What do you hope to gain here, Ānanda:
> That which has been born,
> has become, has been formed,
> and which is of the nature to break up
> —"May that, indeed, not break up!"?
> This thing is just not possible.

Ānanda survived the Buddha by many years, and in the verses left behind in the *Theragāthā*, we hear Ānanda recounting the event and speaking movingly about his loss:

> *Then was my heart seized by terror,*
> *Then did my hair stand on its end,*
> *When he who possessed all goodness,*
> *—Buddha was fully extinguished.*
>
> *All the directions are obscure,*
> *Things are no longer clear for me;*
> *Now that my loving friend is gone,*
> *It seems as if all is darkness.*

*For one whose friend has passed away,
One whose teacher is gone for good,
There is no friend that can compare
With mindfulness of the body.*

*The old ones have all passed away—
I do not fit in with the new.
So now I meditate alone,
Like a bird who has gone to roost.*

(Dīgha Nikāya 16; Theragāthā 1034-1046)

Reflections: Andrew Olendzki

The aging process is almost certain to be accompanied by the gradual loss of acquaintances, friends, and those who are dearly loved by us. It is natural that we want these people to remain with us, and it is just as natural that they will not. The Buddha talked about death with great candor. In his last words to Ānanda we find him speaking, not about rebirth, survival, or a future meeting in a better place, as we might expect, but rather of the inevitability of death. As I understand the profound teachings of Buddhism, complete well-being is to be found within the truths of aging, illness, and death, rather than being dependent on an escape from these.

I think there is a distinction to be made here between the deep feeling of mental pain on one hand, which is as inevitable as the experience of physical pain when the body becomes afflicted, and on the other hand an emotional response of "lamenting," which is likely to be a form of aversion to the pain of loss. The Buddha seems to be telling Ānanda that there is no need to resist the pain, no need to long for things to be other than they are, and that even in the face of tremendous loss, one can feel a sense of balance and well-being. This is liberation *within* conditions, rather than liberation *from* conditions.

Of course Ānanda is only human, and no doubt was unable to absorb the subtlety of this teaching in his moment of distress. Ānanda acutely feels the loss of his dear friend (I have translated *kalyāna-mitta* here as "loving friend" rather than the more familiar "beneficial friend" or "spiritual friend."), and I'm sure many of us can relate to the experience of losing our bearings he describes so vividly. One has a sense of growing alienation and withdrawal in his verses, as the vibrant new Buddhist movement rolls on with new faces, new energy—and without him. I suspect many people, as they grow older, experience a similar sense of the world rolling past them, so to speak, as they participate less directly as its movers and shakers.

By the final verses, however, Ānanda is an arahant, and we need not read his situation pessimistically, as a person "reduced to" meditating alone. Mindfulness of the body, the simple activity of being acutely aware of every micro-episode of lived experience as physical sensations arise and fall in the body, is portrayed as a great friend. It is a celebration of the precious gift of awareness, of sipping mindfully from the cup of life and savoring every nuance of merely being alive. The image I have of a bird in its nest is not of something abandoned or forlorn, but it is a posture of great dignity and centeredness, nestling down into the very heart of things.

Reflections: Mu Soeng

Whether it is a function of the culture of a different time and place, or a definitive marker of "spiritual" cultivation, we find reminders about death and separation as a recurring theme in Buddhist and non-Buddhist literature from ancient India. Within the Buddha's teachings (take the collection of Dhammapada verses, for example), death and separation are embedded in a worldview of impermanence and not-self.

Along with reminders about eventual death come reminders of loss, grief, and the inevitable separation from what is loved and cherished. All teachers have reminded us about our inability to hold on to anything—most of all our inability to hold on to what we cherish most. Teachers also remind us of the need for cultivating equanimity in the face of all this change.

Equanimity itself is a synonym for non-clinging. We all have been conditioned to live life through possessions and accumulations. In an unexamined life, these turn into clinging for what is being possessed and accumulated. Today's sophisticated understanding of human psychology tells us that clinging arises from neediness, and our neediness prevents us from letting go, from being autonomous, from being free.

The Buddha taught that the end of craving and clinging is the end of suffering. Today we know a lot more about the biochemical processes associated with attachment, craving, and addiction. But we still have to train our emotional lives to accept change and loss with a degree of equanimity. This is all the Buddha asked his followers to do. This training is not denial, nor is it nihilism. It is a realistic response to how all phenomena, including those we love and cherish, arise and pass away.

When we look closely at our grieving processes, we find that often grieving is more about ourselves than the object or person that has been lost. In other words, it can be another layer of self-story in the series of stories that continue to reify our sense of an autonomous self. Similarly, our fear of death is the fear of losing this self that we have worked so hard to create. In moments of insight, we discover it all to be a fiction.

Ānanda had to work through his grief at losing his teacher and mentor in a healthy way, since he was not an arahant at the time of the Buddha's *parinibbāna*. Eventually, however, he learned how to discover freedom even in the face of everything slipping away. Similarly, it is possible for all of us to work through our grief and loss in a healthy way—to keep it about what has been lost and what is being mourned. We don't need to deny the grieving that we must do, but we also don't need to make it about ourselves.

Reflections: Gloria Taraniya Ambrosia

Last weekend I was visiting with a friend who is a few years older than me. She asked, "Do you ever think about death?"

150 • Older and Wiser

"Are you kidding?" I laughed. "I'm a Buddhist. We think about death all the time!"

"Doesn't it scare you?"

"Sure it scares me, but what scares me more is pushing it away and pretending it's not going to happen and then having to deal with it in my final moments ... or worse ... not getting it at all and then struggling as I lay dying, grasping to hold on to life."

One of the most painful aspects of caring for my mom in her final days was watching her resist her inevitable demise. It seemed as though it hadn't occurred to her that this was going to happen. Thus, her death surprised her, caught her off guard. As her frailty increased, so did her anxiety.

In Buddhism we have what one might call an easy layaway plan: Die now, go later. Or: wake up now, die easy.

In his first formal teaching, the Buddha went straight to the heart of the matter of living and dying, suffering and release. In the first noble truth, he listed what might be called the harsh realities of this human realm—birth, aging, and death, having to associate with things we don't like, being separated from things we love, not getting what we want. Just as with Ānanda in this sutta, the Buddha invites reflection. "All that is dear and charming" will become otherwise. One can surmise this was not done out of some morbid preoccupation, but rather out of genuine, heartfelt concern for Ānanda's (and our) welfare. He realized we are caught in the delusion that when things are difficult, something must be wrong ... and that death is a great misfortune instead of a natural occurrence. But as evidenced in Ānanda's subsequent writings, once we are no longer repelled by the physical reality of death, our psychological suffering is diminished significantly, if not eliminated altogether.

But a question might remain. Is the Buddha saying that we should not mourn the loss of our loved ones or feel sad at the prospect of our own death? Not at all. Sorrow is a natural response to loss. However, there is a huge difference between wallowing in the experience of loss, and opening the heart to "that which is of the nature to break up." Insight into *anicca, dukkha,* and *anattā* reaches its highest potential as we open to the reality of death. The Buddha encourages us to find the place of peace within these realities so that we are not repeatedly thrown off balance. Ajahn Chah said that for those who don't understand death, life is very confusing. The challenge here is to find a way to let go now, so we can be at peace in that moment when we face our own death.

152 • Older and Wiser

6.2 The Mustard Seed

After flowing-on for a hundred thousand ages,
she evolved in this Buddha-era among gods and men
in a poor family in Sāvatthi.
Her name was Gotami-tissa,
but because her body was very skinny (*kisa*)
she was called 'Skinny Gotami.' (Kisa Gotami)
When she went to her husband's family,
she was scorned [and called] 'daughter of a poor family.'

Then she gave birth to a son,
and with the arrival of the son she was treated with respect.
But that son, running back and forth
and running all around, while playing met his end.
Because of this, sorrow-to-the-point-of-madness arose in her.
She thought: "Before I was one who received only scorn,
but starting from the time of the birth of my son I gained
honor.
These [relatives] will now try to take my son,
in order to expose him outside [in the charnel ground]."

Under the influence of her sorrow-to-the-point-of-madness,
she took the dead corpse on her hip and
wandered in the city from the door of one house to another
[pleading]: "Give medicine to me for my son!"
People reviled her, [saying] "What good is medicine?"
She did not grasp what they were saying.

And then a certain wise man, thinking,
"This woman has had her mind deranged by sorrow for her
son;
the ten-powered [Buddha] will know the medicine for her,"
said: "Mother, having approached the fully awakened one,
ask about medicine for your son."
She went to the *vihāra*
at the time of the teaching of dhamma and said,
"Blessed One, give medicine to me for my son!"

The master, seeing her situation, said,
"Go, having entered the city,
into whatever house has never before experienced any death,
and take from them a mustard seed."

"Very well, Sir," [she replied,]
and glad of mind she entered the city and came to the first house:
"The master has called for a mustard seed
in order to make medicine for my son.
If this house has never before experienced any death,
give me a mustard seed."
"Who is able to count how many have died here?"
"Then keep it. What use is that mustard seed to me?"
And going to a second and a third house,
her madness left her, and her right mind was established
—thanks to the power of the Buddha.

She thought, "This is the way it will be in the entire city.
By means of the Buddha's compassion for my welfare,
this will be what is seen."
And having gained a sense of spiritual urgency from that,
she went out and covered her son in the charnel ground.

She uttered this verse:

> *It's not just a truth for one village or town,*
> *Nor is it a truth for a single family.*
> *But for every world settled by gods [and men]*
> *This indeed is what is true—impermanence.*

And so saying, she went into the presence of the master.
Then the master said to her,
"Have you obtained, Gotami, the mustard seed?"
"Finished, sir, is the matter of the mustard seed," she said.
"You have indeed restored me."

And the master then uttered this verse:

> *A person with a mind that clings,*
> *Deranged, to sons or possessions,*
> *Is swept away by death that comes*

154 • Older and Wiser

—Like mighty flood to sleeping town.
At the conclusion of this verse, confirmed in the fruit of stream-entry,
she asked the master [for permission] to go forth [into the homeless life].
The master allowed her to go forth.
She gave homage to the master by bowing three times,
went to join the community of nuns,
and having gone forth, received her ordination.
It was not long before, through the doing of deeds with careful attention,
she caused her insight to grow ... and she became an arahant.
(Therīgāthā Atthakathā 10.1)

Reflections: Andrew Olendzki

This is one of the more poignant stories found in early Buddhist literature, translated here rather literally to bring out some of the idiom of the original language. It is well known, but there are nuances here that are often overlooked in the more common retellings of the story.

One factor is that Gotami felt scorned by her in-laws on account of her poverty, and that this changed dramatically when she gave birth to a son. (Alas, this ill-treatment of women by their in-laws and masculine bias are still very much alive in India.) Therefore, the loss of her son would also have resulted in a significant loss of status, which may well have contributed to her despair.

Another minor point is that her child was evidently a toddler when he died rather than the infant we usually hear about, since he died after "running back and forth and running all around." This would have given her even more time to bond with him, also intensifying the loss.

The main point of the story, of course, is Gotami's eventual realization that her personal loss is part of a much wider fabric of the human condition. While her grief resulted in a sort of madness, it is insight into the truth of impermanence that enables her to emerge from that madness and restores her to her "right mind." As we have seen before, the theme here is salvation—not from conditions, but within conditions. There is no magic potion made of mustard seeds that can restore her son to life, but there is a way to heal the wounds of her grief and render her whole, even as she loses such an important part of herself. There are so many lessons here for all of us, as we age and lose so much of value.

The Buddha's verse makes the even larger point that we are all not quite in our right minds about anything, to the extent that we relate to the world through craving and clinging. How many things, large and small, do we clutch in our arms as we walk from place to place, pleading for something to be other than it is? Gotami is lamenting the loss of her son; might we not on occasion experience sorrow-to-the-point-of-madness regarding a prized possession, a cherished belief, a habitual behavior, or a diminution of our sense of self? What will it take to transport these willingly to the charnel ground and cover them with earth? The doing of deeds with careful attention?

I'm glad this story ends well. I think Gotami is able to live out her life with a deep sense of peace because she learns to take a wider view on the great matters of life and death. Looked at from the narrow perspective of "me," it all seems so unbearably tragic. But looking broadly over the whole expanse of the human condition, a view we are often able to access from the perspective of age, a dignified ending completes, and possibly even perfects, a human life well lived.

Reflections: Mu Soeng

I find this story to be not only one of the most compelling and poignant in the entire Pāli Canon, but also a classic example of skillful means of a teacher. In many ways, it sets the Buddha apart from his contemporary teachers who claimed to heal a person through their powers of omniscience, while here the healing is

156 • Older and Wiser

done entirely through self-understanding. Its significance also lies in the formation and shaping of the later Mahāyāna tradition as a vehicle of skillful means. The famous Lotus Sutra is a paean to skillful means, and a tradition of *ekāyana* ("one vehicle") grew in medieval Japanese Buddhism, especially, on the premise that all of Buddha's teachings are one vehicle: the perfection of skillful means.

The perfection or training or accomplishment in skillful means is naturally grounded in compassion. Gotami had been scorned by others in the village for her desperate wish to restore her son back to life. But the Buddha embraced her sorrow, so to speak, and responded with compassion. In this story, the Buddha's compassion is encapsulated not in any abstract reasoning or argument, but discerning in this moment an appropriate remedy for Gotami's situation. More than most stories in the Pāli suttas, the response of the Buddha here is etiological—the diagnosis by a medical doctor of a malady and the offering of a quick remedy.

Gotami's story is reminiscent of the famous dialogue in the *Mahabharata*, the great Indian epic:

Yaksha: What is the greatest wonder in the world?

Yudhishthira: Every day men see others called to their death, yet those who remain live as if they were immortal.

As Andrew clarifies in his reflections above, there may have been many reasons for Gotami to go insane in her wish to restore her son back to life: both familial and social, but the lesson remains for the rest of us: how do we internalize our own death, as well as the deaths of those who are near and dear to us?

It is natural to feel sorrow and sadness for such a loss, yet it is equally unnatural to go clinically mad in our sorrow and sadness, like Gotami seems to have done. It seems to me that we respect our dead most when we are *proportional* in our sorrow and sadness, not when we go overboard.

This proportionality of emotional responses is what the Middle Way of the Buddha represents to me. The proportionality is equally necessary and appropriate in our enjoyment processes as it is in our grieving processes. When our enjoyment is self-contained and moderate, it is nourishing, just as the self-containment of sorrow and sadness is respectful of our dead. When we go overboard in either situation, it's more about our personal mental health than our capacity for sorrow or enjoyment.

Kisa Gotami's story is paradigmatically inspiring for generations of Buddhist practitioners. Many have found in the story an inspiration for adopting an existential posture in dealing with the sorrows and joys of the world. Let us hope each one of us can adopt the same existential posture.

Reflections: Gloria Taraniya Ambrosia

Gotami's story metaphorically describes the progression from delusion to insight through which we all must pass. For many years (lifetimes!) we tend to put a lot of stock in worldly aims and values. We bolster ourselves with short-term gratification and suffer the highs and lows that necessarily accompany our investments in the world. But sooner or later the realities of impermanence, unsatisfactoriness, and non-self reveal themselves in one way or another and—if our karma is ripe enough to allow us to follow the guidance of our wise and benevolent teacher, the Buddha—we turn toward these realities instead of running away. With eyes wide open, we begin to see through the old ways with their ankle-deep gratification and embark more fully on the path of practice. Thus, we enjoy a reversal of fortune. There is a way to happiness; it's just not where we thought it was.

Gotami's story offers great fodder for contemplation. Perhaps we haven't lost a child or suffered a dramatic decline in social status because of that loss, but perhaps we are advanced enough in years to have experienced the death of parents and friends, as well as diminished status in a society that sees its senior citizens more as dead weight than a valued resource of experience and wisdom. Faced with devastating losses, Gotami appears to have lost her way. Indeed, the sutta implies that she has gone mad with grief. Perhaps she has. Or perhaps Gotami's story is simply nudging us to open our hearts so fully to the pain of the human experience—even to the brink of madness—that we feel the utter hopelessness of finding peace in *saṃsāra* and, thereby, turn our sights towards *nibbāna*. How deeply must we feel the pain of delusion before we release our attachment to the world?

This story also reminds us that what may seem like a great misfortune, if experienced with wise attention and reflection, can be the event that sparks the flame of insight. Gotami suffered a great loss—not only the loss of her child, but also the loss of her status and role in society. These apparently unfortunate events turned out to be the experiences that moved her to go forth into homelessness and to eventually realize arahantship. We can derive great inspiration from the depth of her pain, her courage in facing it, and her insight.

Finally, Gotami's story tells us that true freedom is not found in successfully manipulating or rearranging the pieces on a board game, such that we optimize our lives according to social norms. Rather, freedom involves moving beyond the arena of the world altogether. What's the value in realizing worldly status or success when everything and everyone is subject to impermanence? What really is worthy of our attention?

In the *Dhammapada* we read: "Better a single day of life perceiving how things rise and fall than to live out a century yet not perceive their rise and fall." (Dhp. 113)

6.3 Unbearable Grief

In one of the more tragic stories of the Pāli Canon, a well-born young woman runs off with a family servant and lives happily in another region, eventually giving birth to two sons. Then in a series of freakish catastrophes, she loses everything and goes mad with grief and despair. This is where we pick up the story ...

> In that moment
> she did not perceive that
> the clothes she was wearing were falling off.
> A madness born of grief had fallen upon her,
> and such was its form:
>
>> *Both of my sons have met their end,*
>> *My husband—dead in the jungle;*
>> *Mother, father, and brother, all*
>> *Burned on a single funeral pyre.*
>
> —she staggered around wailing.
>
> From then on,
> because her clothes kept falling off, and she
> roamed around (*ācāra*) with fallen clothing (*paṭa*),
> the name "Paṭācārā" arose.
>
> When seen by men:
> "Go away, you mad person!"
> Some threw rubbish at her head,
> others hurled mud,
> still others threw lumps of dirt.
>
> The master was at Jetavana,
> amid a great gathering,
> seated, teaching the dhamma.
> He saw her staggering around like that,
> and discerning her ripeness for understanding,
> he made for the gate of the *vihāra*

where she was coming.

When the gathering saw her, they said:
"This is a mad person!
Do not allow her to come here."
The Buddha, saying "Do not prevent her,"
was standing nearby when she came around:

"Regain your presence of mind, sister," he said.

Then, through the power of the Buddha,
she regained her presence of mind.
Realizing that her clothes were falling off,
and restoring her self-respect and social conscience,
she sat down, squatting on her haunches.

A man threw her a covering robe.
Wrapped in that
she approached the master and,
venerating him with a five-fold prostration, said:

"Protect me, sir!
One son of mine was seized by a hawk,
and one was swept away by water.
My husband lies dead in the forest,
while my mother, father, and brother
were killed by a collapsing building
and burned upon a single funeral pyre."

Thus she poured out the causes of her grief.

The master gave this teaching:

"Do not think, Paṭācārā,
that you have come into the safe presence
of one who can protect you.
Just as you shed tears now for these loved ones
because they have been marked by death,
so too in the on-flow without beginning or end
you've shed more tears for loved ones,
because of death, than all the water
of the four great oceans."

—he then uttered this stanza:

> *The water of the four oceans is trifling*
> *Compared to the vast ocean of tears that are shed*
> *From grief for those who've been touched by pain.*
> *What work, mother, are you now neglecting?*

Thus, with the master's speaking
a talk on the simile of immeasurable limit,
her grief became lighter to bear.

Then, knowing that her grief had become lighter,
he gave this teaching:

"Paṭācārā, for one passing to a world beyond,
it is simply not possible
for sons and all the rest
to be a safety, a shelter, a refuge.

Even in the present they are not such.
Yet, by clarifying one's conduct,
a path leading to *nibbāna*
might be accomplished by the wise."

Then he taught the dhamma with these stanzas:

> *Sons provide no sanctuary;*
> *Nor do fathers or family.*
> *For those who are facing the end,*
> *There is no safety in kinship.*

> *Knowing the power of this truth,*
> *the wise one, restrained with virtue,*
> *quickly clears a way on the path*
> *leading onward to nibbāna.*

After this teaching, Paṭācārā
attained the fruit of stream-entry
and asked the master to go forth.
The master led her into the presence
of the nuns, and had her go forth.

(Therīgāthā Aṭṭhakathā 112-116)

162 • Older and Wiser

Reflections: Andrew Olendzki

I like to go back to some of the well-known stories in the Pāli texts, such as this one, and re-translate the telling of the story as literally as possible. One thing this does is bring out the power and clarity of the literature that is often lost when it is smoothed out to sound more familiar in English. In some places the idiom is a bit awkward, but in other ways it brings out details and nuances of the story that might otherwise get mislaid in translation. Three things stand out here.

The first is the phrase the Buddha uses to help Paṭācārā emerge from her despair and recover her right mind. He actually uses the word for mindfulness, which is *sati*. I render it "Regain your presence of mind," in order to clarify that I do not think the Buddha is giving her meditation instruction, but we could even more literally say, "Regain your mindfulness." This is not to say that going on a mindfulness meditation retreat is recommended for people who are overwhelmed with grief (it is not), but I do think the use of this word is significant.

Notice that Paṭācārā's distress is linked to the re-telling of her story. We hear her recite it in a formal stanza, perhaps over and over to passersby, and then she pours it out again to the Buddha in prose. Mindfulness is all about being attentive to present moment sensory experience, and if she is fully present to the moment, she cannot be simultaneously recalling her past losses. This breaks the momentum of the grief, if only for an instant, which is apparently enough for her to snap out of being absorbed by her sorrow. It is as though she were stabbing herself with a second arrow (See 4:2 *Stabbed by One Arrow—Not Two*) every time she relived her trauma, and only stopped doing so when she became mindful. This is not a cure, but it is a first step in the right direction.

Next we hear the Buddha quite unexpectedly saying that he is not one who can protect her from harm. We are used to hearing about going to the Buddha for refuge, and such safety is promised by other religious figures, such as Jesus, but the Buddha's teaching here is not soft and reassuring. It is the same approach that worked for Skinny Gotami with her dead son (*The Mustard Seed, #6.2*): All beings pass away according to their karma; understanding this first noble truth is necessary for the healing of grief.

Finally, we see that the Buddha, having rendered her grief lighter and somewhat easier to bear, goes on to speak compassionately to her of a way leading beyond all suffering. This diligent "work" begins with clarifying one's conduct, and leads, as we know, through mental development and the eventual deepening of wisdom.

Paṭācārā joins the order of nuns, becomes an arahant, and for many years to come is a great leader of the female monastic community, helping many other women to emerge from their grief and set out on the path leading onward …

Reflections: Mu Soeng

Though the storyline in this poem seems highly compressed, the healing of Paṭācārā might have been a much more drawn-out affair. As with Kisa Gotami, this story speaks eloquently of Buddha's willingness to work with social outcasts, such as seemingly crazy people like Paṭācārā. Notice how his own disciples were not willing to interact with her when Paṭācārā appeared in the vicinity of Jetavana, and even tried to prevent the Buddha from seeing her.

The Buddha offered Paṭācārā "tough love." The subtext of him saying that he could not be a refuge for her reads to me as a declaration that he was not a miracle worker who could bring her dead children or husband back to life, if that's what she was looking for. In asking her to "regain her mindfulness," the Buddha is essentially asking Paṭācārā to regain that basic hardwired awareness each human being is born with and which is prior to all events of joy and sorrow. This is our essential humanity, which we can access at any time, if we make the effort to become free of the hold of the events of joy and sorrow. In asking Paṭācārā to regain her mindfulness, the Buddha is essentially asking her to recover her humanity.

It is the same recovery we negotiate when we go on a meditation retreat and work with a skillful teacher. Our core awareness is part of the neural network in our brains, and we need not glamorize it as anything mystical or extraordinary. Paṭācārā's recovery began in earnest when she was able, under the Buddha's guidance, to see that her story, monumentally full of grief though it was, was still a story. That realization was the first step in a long journey for Paṭācārā on the path to arahantship.

Paṭācārā's realization is also our realization. We, too, can see that *dukkha* arises when we are held captive by our stories, our clinging to them, and our unwillingness to let them go. Still, in the midst of all these stories and their drama, there is a pristine awareness that sees, as if from outside, the twirls and turns of all the drama being played out.

The Buddha could not put Paṭācārā directly in touch with this pristine awareness, and no teacher can do it for us either. For some, getting in touch with it may be long, hard work, but it is through this core awareness that we see the limitations of the stories being played out in our lives. Paṭācārā had to learn how to hold her story, and we need to do the same.

Reflections: Gloria Taraniya Ambrosia

In this teaching the Buddha is saying that family and friends do not bring safety, refuge, or shelter—now, yesterday, or tomorrow. To think of them in this way will potentially bring great hardship into our lives. As the Buddha told Paṭācārā, there is no protection from the pain associated with attachment in relationships. All of us have "shed more tears for loved ones because of death than all the water of the four great oceans."

At first reading, this may seem harsh or severe. As householders, many of us would say that our greatest treasure is our family and friends. We might even go so far as to say that this is what life is all about—that caring for loved ones and being nourished in our relationships is why we get up every day—and that the potential pain of loss is a necessary by-product.

So how do we make sense of the Buddha's teaching to Paṭācārā? Perhaps he is not so much saying that family and friends are not important, as he is pointing us in the direction of what is. Paṭācārā's story and the Buddha's teaching to her encourage us to scrutinize and challenge our thinking, as well as to redirect our focus. Attachment in relationships can actually be a diversion from what is truly important: "What work are you neglecting?" he asks.

Years ago I was present at a Buddhist blessing ceremony for a couple who was getting married. I was struck by how the monk did not encourage them to cling to one another as in conventional ceremonies. Rather he clearly identified such clinging as one of the possible burdens they would likely bear as a couple. The sole purpose of coming together, he said, was to be a support to each other in the process of waking up. He encouraged them to focus on this shared goal, to do their best to nourish each other's aspiration, to bear each other's unfinished parts, and to use the relationship to learn about non-attachment. If they do this, he said, their life together would be good and beneficial, and the potential for hardship would be diminished.

The same blessing might be given to parents at the birth of a child or to loved ones at the deathbed of a relative or friend. These transitions that characterize a normal human lifetime—birth, marriage, death—call for us to reflect on the deeper meaning of life and to contemplate what is truly important. As the Buddha said to Paṭācārā: "For one passing to a world beyond, it is simply not possible for sons [and others] to be a safety, a shelter, a refuge." They are not such now, nor will they ever be. But by clarifying our conduct, we might realize the goal of liberation. It's about focusing our energies on the true heart's release.

With these words ... and with her commensurate insight Paṭācārā's grief became lighter to bear. Thus freed, she moved beyond refuge in attachment to worldly relationships and proclaimed her faith in the only true refuge—the Buddha, Dhamma, and Sangha. She realized stream-entry and went forth into the holy life.

6.4 The Soothing of Grief

This tender poem of loss and recovery was (probably) composed by Paṭācārā, one of the leading women of the Buddha's order of nuns. Born the daughter of a wealthy banker, Paṭācārā fell in love with one of her father's servants and ran off to live happily with him in a forest hamlet. Then, through a series of tragic accidents, she lost first her husband, then two sons, and finally her parents and brother.

Wandering destitute, naked, and mad with grief, she in time met the Buddha face to face, who showed her kindness when others would scorn her. She heard his teaching, joined the order of nuns, and went on to become one of the awakened arahants, or worthy ones. Paṭācārā helped many other women who were overcome by grief regain their sanity and quench the pain of their loss, including Skinny Gotami of the mustard seed story.

> *"My son!" you weep, for one whose path*
> *You do not comprehend at all—*
> *Whether he's coming or going.*
> *From where has that son of yours come?*
>
> *And yet for one whose path you know ...*
> *For him you do not grieve at all—*
> *Whether he's coming or going.*
> *Such is the nature of creatures.*
>
> *Uninvited, he came from there;*
> *Unpermitted, he's gone from here.*
> *And having come from who knows where,*
> *He lived for but a few short days.*
>
> *But though gone from here by one (path),*
> *He goes from there by another.*
> *Departed, with a human form,*
> *He will go flowing on and on.*
>
> *As he has come, so has he gone.*

168 • Older and Wiser

What is there here to grieve about?

My thorn, indeed, has been removed!
Buried in the heart, so hard to see.
That grief which had overcome me—
Grief for my son—has been dispelled.

Today the thorn has been removed.
Without hunger, I've become quenched.
To Buddha, Dhamma, and Sangha,
I go to the sage for refuge.

(Therīgāthā 127-132)

Reflections: Andrew Olendzki

Although this poem is directed particularly at the loss of a son, I think its sentiment and teaching extend easily to all those we love and lose. The emphasis is upon the process of coming and going, on what in ancient India was called "flowing on and on" (the word for this is *saṃsāra,* based on the verb "to flow"). It is a fundamentally natural process: "Such is the nature of creatures." Our suffering in the face of losing someone we care for is rooted in our not understanding the larger picture, and in our trying to hold on to something that by nature flows and is thus ungraspable.

In the Buddha's day it was widely accepted that this life is only a way station in a larger journey, as each person is born into the human condition and then passes away to another state according to their karma. Some destinations are better than this one, others far more unfortunate. It was never spelled out exactly how all this works, and was largely a folk belief held on faith. Alas it is the same for us today—there is no explanation or proof for this notion of rebirth, and if we have this belief now it must also be largely on faith. However, there is also no compelling evidence for the only two other possibilities: either that one lives forever in another world or that the lights go out forever and there is nothing.

I'm personally agnostic on the whole issue, but in times of great loss I find it comforting to think of life and death as a natural flow, like everything else in nature. I'm guessing it is naive to hope for personal survival, but entirely okay to envision our lives as part of a larger process. As to the poet's question: "What is there here to grieve about?" the Buddha's answer seems to be simply that we will suffer in direct proportion to our grasping. If we cannot change the way things are, the skill of life becomes learning how to feel deep love and care for what is flowing through our fingers, even while letting it go.

The thorn removed from Paṭācārā's heart is not the love she holds for her son, but the attachment to wanting things to be different than they are. Her son, like all beings, was not an entity that existed, as much as a unique process that occurred. The gift is given, without our asking; the gift is returned, without our permission. Each moment of awareness is also a gift—that will surely be returned one day. We are all just "flowing on" from one moment to another, and how well we flourish while we are here has to do with how freely we can flow. The love that clings is a source of pain; the love that surrenders is a source of poignant beauty. Paṭācārā is telling us, from her own personal experience, that deep love is compatible with a deep acceptance of change.

Reflections: Mu Soeng

I must admit that I find the language of this poem to be fairly inaccessible. It alludes to certain ideas (of karma and rebirth) that require an "insider" understanding of what is being talked about. I would like to think that Paṭācārā's story points to a deep knowing that allowed her, even in the midst of tremendous grief and loss, to comprehend that loss and death are natural recurrences in the human world.

This inherent deep knowing is of particular interest to Buddhist practitioners, since it is the basis of aspiration for liberation. My own personal experience is that even in the midst of our greatest grief or greatest joy, there is a core awareness that stands outside of the experience of the moment and is able to look at it from outside. This core awareness seems to be hardwired into our system and pops out from time to time. I want to be very clear and make sure that I am not calling this core awareness anything other than a neural process hardwired into our cognitive apparatus. I am tempted to call it part of the reptilian part of the brain, but it needs to be languaged out in more comprehensive ways than are possible here.

What's most interesting, however, is that Paṭācārā was able to harmonize her grievous situation with this core awareness. Zen tradition has called this harmonizing of core awareness in the midst of our most intense experience "sudden awakening," and that's what I see happening here: Paṭācārā suddenly awoke to the supreme fact that life and death are just two happenings in the flowing of the great river of *saṃsāra*. She was able to step outside of her personal grief and loss to have a more cosmic view, if you will, of how it all works: all who are born must die. This was Paṭācārā's liberation/sudden awakening.

The lesson to be learned, I guess, is that this core awareness allows us to see the universal processes at work in our personal stories of loss and grief. Yes, our personal story of sickness, aging, and dying (of ourselves and those near and dear to us) is difficult and stressful, but each one of us has the same wisdom faculty as Paṭācārā to also see the impersonal nature of those processes.

The Zen template of sudden awakening is always paired with "gradual cultivation." While sudden awakening is not such a rare a phenomenon, gradual cultivation is a much harder task to accomplish. That Paṭācārā was able to let go of her personal grief and commit herself to gradual cultivation was her incredible achievement. Most people cannot do it so easily, but it can be done. Paṭācārā's story is also a universal exhortation: Even in the midst of our most difficult situations, we can step out, see it from the outside, and deal with the after effects through wisdom and compassion, without losing our sense of balance and equanimity.

Reflections: Gloria Taraniya Ambrosia

Paṭācārā lost everyone who was dear to her—suddenly, violently, and all within a short period of time. Thankfully, that's not how things usually unfold. But her story serves as an effective backdrop for teachings (1) on the importance of insight into impermanence—not only as a key component of awakening, but also as a way ultimately to put an end to the experience of grief—and (2) on the importance of contemplating rebirth. One might include a third theme implicit in this excerpt, which involves recognizing that no worldly relationship can be a refuge for us. Only insight will clear the obstacles on our path to freedom.

At first glance, the encouragement to transcend grief may seem shocking and confusing. Aren't we trying to open to painful feeling, to embrace the realities of sickness, aging, and death … and all the pain that accompanies that embrace? Is the Buddha now saying that we should somehow transcend such natural responses as grief? Frankly, that may not be very attractive or desirable.

It helps to realize that there is a gradual process involved in waking up to impermanence. We can say, "Oh, I get it. Everything is impermanent and that's just the way it is." But what does it really mean to penetrate this reality? Perhaps our first task is to be with the natural feeling of sorrow/grief … and to learn how not to wallow in it so that we can more easily see its impermanent nature. As we slowly discover how all phenomena move through, we come to a place that so fully recognizes the natural order of things that the heart no longer whimpers in the presence of it.

As to the theme of rebirth … at the beginning of the poem, we learn that the Buddha encouraged Paṭācārā to step outside her preoccupation with the *fact* that we are born and we die, and to focus instead on understanding what drives these cycles. We applaud birth and grieve death, and yet we don't even know or understand where we come from or where we go. As children we ask, "Where did I come from?" and

172 • Older and Wiser

thoughtful parents stumble in their reply. We ask, "Where do we go when we die?" Answers that satisfied us when we were five—"Grandma is in heaven now."—fall short of the mark as we mature. Here we see how the Buddha encouraged Paṭācārā to move beyond immature levels of concern and to ask more penetrative questions.

As we contemplate the possibility of rebirth, many of us conclude that it makes sense and we trust the Buddha's teaching— even if we have not developed the powers of mind that secure that knowing. We might even feel a twisted relief. *"Departed, with a human form, He will go flowing on and on. As he has come, so has he gone. What is there here to grieve about?"* With these words ... and with her commensurate insight ... Paṭācārā expelled the grief from her heart. Free, she moved beyond refuge in attachment to worldly relationships and proclaimed her faith in the only true refuge—the Buddha, Dhamma, and Sangha.

7. Practice

7.1 The Simile of the Heartwood

A person goes forth with confidence
from the home life into homelessness, thinking:
'I am subject to birth, aging, and death,
to sorrow, lamentation, pain, grief, and despair;
I am subject to suffering, the prey of suffering.
Surely an ending of this whole mass of suffering can be known.'

When he has gone forth thus, he acquires gain, honor, and renown.

He is pleased with that gain, honor, and renown,
and considers his intention to be fulfilled.
On account of this he lauds himself and disparages others thus:
'I have gain, honor, and renown,
but these others are unknown, of no account.'

So he arouses no desire to act further;
he makes no effort for the realization of those other states
that are higher and more sublime than gain, honor, and renown.

He hangs back and slackens.

> I say that this person is like the man needing heartwood,
> who comes to a great tree standing possessed of heartwood,
> and passing over its heartwood, its sapwood, its inner bark, and its outer bark and twigs,
> cuts off its leaves and takes them away thinking they are heartwood;
> So whatever it was he had to make with heartwood,
> his purpose will not be served.

[The text repeats, as other men successively attain virtue, concentration, knowledge and vision, and then a number of refined meditative states. The

metaphor is applied to each of these as the twigs, outer bark, inner bark, and sapwood of the tree.]

> Another man goes forth with confidence...
> and also acquires gain, honor, and renown [...*etc.*].
> But he is not pleased with that gain, honor, and renown [...*etc.*],
> and does not consider his intention to be fulfilled.
> He does not, on account of it, laud himself and disparage others.
> Instead, he arouses desire to act further,
> and he makes an effort for the realization of those other states that are higher and more sublime than gain, honor, and renown [...*etc.*];
> He does not hang back and slacken.
> And his taints are destroyed by seeing with wisdom [*i.e., he attains awakening*].
>
> I say that this person is like a man needing heartwood, seeking heartwood, wandering in search of heartwood,
> who comes to a great tree standing possessed of heartwood,
> and passing over its leaves and twigs, its outer bark, inner bark, and sapwood,
> cuts out its heartwood and takes it away, knowing it is heartwood.
> So whatever it was he had to make with heartwood,
> his purpose will be served.
> This holy life does not have gain, honor, and renown as its goal,
> nor the attainment of virtue, concentration, or knowledge and vision,
> nor does it have various refined meditative states as its goal.
> It is unshakeable deliverance of mind
> that is the goal of this holy life, its heartwood, and its end.
>
> (*Cūḷa Sāropama Sutta, Majjhima Nikāya* 30)

Reflections: Andrew Olendzki

This simile points out how easy it is to fall short of all we are capable of by succumbing to the allure of lesser accomplishments. Perhaps these men settled for less because each achievement was so gratifying, or because too much more work was required to go further, or perhaps from not understanding what was peripheral and what was central. The Buddha uses this image to encourage his monks and nuns to strive for liberation in this lifetime, but we might also make use of it as an aid to approaching retirement.

When people in ancient India left home in their senior years to wander forth into the homeless life, it was to go as far as they possibly could with their own spiritual development. Is this such an unreasonable ideal for us to aspire toward today? What if we endeavored to understand the meaning of our lives as much as possible, to understand the meaning of life itself as much as humanly possible, to so deeply comprehend it all that we become imperturbable in the face of any alteration, any affliction, any loss? Is this really beyond our reach?

It may be enough for many people to revel in the benefits of not having to go to work every day, of living on a fixed income, and of having their time no longer structured by others. This is indeed a fortunate situation to inhabit, and there are many still on the treadmill who would envy such a state. But there may be others who aspire to more than this, to using their new-found freedom to learn new skills, to improve themselves in various ways, or to seek out experiences that were previously inaccessible. This too is admirable, and we respect those who make such decisions for their enthusiasm and energy. Might one aspire even further?

Some will want to help others, by taking some of the burdens off their children and helping to raise their grandchildren, for example, or by volunteering in their communities or attending their friends who need assistance. Such activities nurture qualities of generosity and kindness and compassion—a worthy goal for one's senior years. Still others may be in a position to dedicate much of their time and energy to meditation and the study of the Dhamma, attending silent retreats, listening to the teachings of wise elders, and working on understanding the nature of their own mind and body in a deep and nuanced way. Surely this is work approaching the very center.

But the heartwood? This entails a deep and abiding transformation. One not only understands the teachings but embodies them, enacts them, and in a sense becomes them. I hear the Buddha exhorting us all to aspire beyond what is gratifying, beyond what is worthwhile, beyond even what is gracious, noble, and selfless. What is that unshakable deliverance of mind? What would it take to be so deeply shaped by wisdom that one becomes a model for all a human being is capable of … all that is best in human nature? I don't know. But I hope there are some in the world who will find out someday, before they pass away.

Reflections: Mu Soeng

The last lines of this passage on the simile of the Heartwood ("This holy life does not have gain, honor, and renown as its goal.") is one of the most remarkable teachings in a lifetime of many remarkable teachings. And the Buddha walked his talk: for 45 years, barefoot through forests and towns, owning nothing but a simple ochre wrap around his body.

Surely, gaining liberation has nothing to do with gaining worldly rewards of fame and wealth. Buddhist history (as well as the history of every religion out there) is littered with teachers, prophets, and messiahs who did not listen to their own voices and ended up diving into the deep end of greed, aversion, and delusion. They turned out to be like those who just walked away with some leaves from the tree, as the simile says.

The Zen tradition reminds us that life and death are both momentous and insignificant at the same time. It talks about the "Great Effort" which seems to mirror the Right Effort of the eightfold path. The effort is not to be directed toward attaining fame and wealth, or even becoming a "holy" person. What, after all, is holy about a person, unless, as the myths tell us, you are able to part the seas or fly into the air like Superman?

Right Effort, as cultivation of wholesome mindfulness, is still necessary in the next moment. Whatever happens in this moment, there's still the next moment, and the next moment after the next moment. Some of these next moments are moments of what we call life, and one of those moments will be a moment of death (or whatever we choose to call it). The whole point of the "unshakeable deliverance of mind" is to meet that moment with courage and dignity, not with fear and trembling. But since that moment remains forever unknown (until it comes around) all we can do is bring wholesome mindfulness to this moment, to the ending and renouncing of greed, hatred, and delusion. This is the great work of life and death.

It seems to me that it is humanly possible to aspire to this Great Effort at any time in our life, but especially in our retirement years. Each one of us can recalibrate the degree of "renouncement" this simile is calling for within the framework of attending to the present moment in a balanced way. The "balance" we bring to attending to this moment is what the Right Effort or the Great Effort is. It does not require walking barefoot through the street. All it requires is an internalization of the fact that in each moment we are utterly alone with the stories we have created about ourselves and for ourselves, and we live and die with these stories in each moment. True renunciation is holding these stories in a balanced way, such that we can let them go and not let the stories hold us in their grip. This is the work of psychological homelessness at its best. This is the great work of Going Forth.

Reflections: Gloria Taraniya Ambrosia

There are a couple of useful reflections in this sutta. The first has to do with recognizing the tendency to settle for superficial forms of letting go, to think that outer renunciation is all we have to do. One might feel good, for example, because one has put aside the common material trappings of our culture. Such people might even boast about it and privately think themselves better than others. "I'm a Buddhist. Look at how non-attached I am." You may have met people like this! They go through the motions but fail to take the practice to heart. As the sutta says, they make "no effort for the realization of ... higher [states], the states that truly merit honor and renown." The work of practice hasn't really been taken up.

Interestingly, this sutta is not necessarily an indictment on this. The Buddha doesn't seem to be overly critical of the first monk. I think it's more of a wake-up call. The Buddha points to major pitfalls—the tendency to look to the outer world for satisfaction, to settle for superficial rewards, to get caught up in worldly measures of happiness and success. Like the first monk, we may feel we don't have to do anything else for the remainder of our lives, a view strongly supported by much of our culture: Retirement ... a time to do nothing. But is this the way we want to live? Do we want to bide our time and wait to die? Implicitly, the Buddha encourages us to seek the profound rewards that only insight into the truths of Dhamma can provide. Don't float on the surface waters—dare to plunge into the depths. The rewards are far greater!

The second useful reflection has to do with making full use of inner renunciation by, in our case, recognizing the great value of our senior years. We are not monastics. However, in our senior years ... because we are free of many of the demands of the home life ... we have conditions that are not unlike those of the men and women who have donned the ochre robes and taken up the holy life. As older householders, we are more free and unencumbered than ever before to follow our true heart's aspiration, to awaken in this very life, to realize the "unshakeable deliverance of mind." And we have the wisdom garnered through many years of practice. Thank goodness we have lived long enough to use that wisdom and to cultivate even more.

In one of the more famous Ajahn Chah stories, he admonished a woman who put too much emphasis on intellectual concepts instead of benefiting from practice in her own heart. He said, "You, madam, are like one who keeps hens in her yard and goes around picking up the chicken droppings instead of the eggs." Squandering our senior years would be like picking up the droppings.

7.2 The Parable of Six Creatures

A person who has not established mindfulness of the body dwells with a limited mind. Such a person does not understand as it really is the liberation of the mind, the liberation brought on by wisdom, in which toxic, unwholesome mental states that have arisen entirely cease. Why? Because they are attached to what is pleasing and repelled by what is unpleasing.

Imagine that a person were to catch six creatures (a snake, a crocodile, a bird, a dog, a jackal, and a monkey), bind each with a strong rope, tie the rope ends together in a single knot, and then let go. Those six creatures, each of a different habitat, would struggle to return to the place they were most comfortable: the snake would try to go to the anthill, the crocodile to the river, the bird to the sky, the dog to the village, the jackal to the charnel ground, and the monkey to the forest. And when these six hungry creatures would get tired, they would surrender to the power of whichever creature was the strongest of them.

It is the same situation for a person whose mindfulness of the body is undeveloped. Each of the senses (the eye, the ear, the nose, the tongue, the body, and the mind), struggles to reach pleasing objects, while unpleasing objects are considered repulsive and are avoided.

A person who has established mindfulness of the body dwells with an unlimited mind. Such a person understands as it really is the liberation of the mind, the liberation brought on by wisdom, in which toxic, unwholesome mental states that have arisen entirely cease. Why? Because they are no longer attached to what is pleasing and repelled by what is unpleasing.

Imagine that a person, having caught six creatures as above, were to tie them all to a single post. At first each would struggle to go where it was most comfortable, but eventually the creatures would tire and settle down next to one another beside the post.

182 • Older and Wiser

It is the same situation for a person whose mindfulness of the body is developed. The senses no longer struggle to reach pleasing objects, and unpleasing objects are not considered repulsive and to be avoided.

The six creatures in this story are a metaphor for the six senses, while the post is a metaphor for mindfulness of the body.

(Samyutta Nikāya 35:247)

Reflections: Andrew Olendzki

This story turns on its head our ordinary notion of freedom. We are accustomed to thinking of freedom as the ability to do what we want, overcoming any obstacles that might prevent us from fulfilling our desires. The Buddha regards wanting itself as a restraint upon our minds, and thus defines freedom as the ability to no longer be driven by desire. It is freedom from want, rather than freedom to want.

Equally counter-intuitive is the notion that this unlimiting of the mind is attained through the discipline of binding awareness to a particular object, as one does in the practice of mindfulness of the body. When the ear is intrigued by the sound of a chirping bird, or the nose is distracted by the smell of lunch, or the mind is seduced by a happy memory—we are asked to let go of the promise of each particular sensual gratification and return to awareness of physical sensations, even if they co-arise with feeling tones of discomfort. When mindfulness is truly established, it is attended by a quality of mind that is profoundly interested in the sensation, but which is grounded in equanimity and thus unconcerned whether it is pleasant or unpleasant. Instead of being reflexively hijacked by habits of pursuing pleasure and avoiding pain, the more mature mind is now able to see a broader swathe of experience with a wider emotional range.

I suspect this is similar to some of the changes that accompany retirement. No longer automatically pushed and pulled as relentlessly by the eight worldly things (gain & loss, fame & shame, praise & blame, pleasure & pain), one develops the ability to embrace the whole range of the human experience with a greater sense of context and poignancy. We now know, deeply and intuitively, that avoiding pain and loss, for example, is not possible. Instead of trying vainly to push it away, we might bring our attention to bear directly upon it and explore the nuanced textures of the experience. We might find as much meaning in sorrow as in joy, in discomfort as in ease, in limitation as in empowerment. What each of the six animals lost in their unrequited longing for home was compensated for by the tranquility of lying down at ease in the present moment.

Mindfulness liberates the mind from wanting. There is plenty of time for aspirations, regrets, reminiscences, and complaints. But in those moments when you sit at the root of a tree or an empty place and "establish the presence of mindfulness," as the discourse puts it, the mind is temporarily free from all that. One learns to see what is happening, in any moment, as the given reality it is. It is, for now, not about what we like or don't like, what we want or don't want; it is just about seeing it as it actually is.

What wears us out is the struggle to reach pleasing objects and avoid what we deem repulsive. These toxic mental states cause our suffering by binding the mind with attachment to a particular desire. At a certain stage of life, we are more able to let go of such limitations, allow things to be just as they are, and settle down peacefully in full awareness of just what is happening.

Reflections: Mu Soeng

The six "hungry" creatures of the parable seem to be the story of our human existence. Their hunger compels them to seek their preprogrammed habitats without regard to whether or not those habitats are skillful. Our human programming works in similar ways: unfulfilled, unsatisfied, feeling incomplete, we are always looking for that next thing that we hope will complete us. And then something funny happens. Without our being aware of it, our grasping for that next thing becomes a habit force and takes over how we make decisions about our need for satisfaction in this moment, as well as in the grand scheme of things we call life. Under the impact of a perpetual sense of incompleteness, we remain confused about what we truly need or want.

In the parable, each creature, when captured, struggles to go back to the habitat in which it is most comfortable. In our human condition, too, the line between the habit force and being truly comfortable in the habitat becomes blurred. We mistake the habit force for an indicator of who we truly are. The inevitable pull of this habit force is to mold us into a consumer both of the pleasant (through grasping) and the unpleasant (through aversion). The subsequent stretch from consumer to addict is not all that much of a leap. The dilemma of our lives is whether to remain addicted to acquisition (of pleasure) or avoidance (of the painful).

Unlike the six creatures of the parables, we humans have the power to see that our habit forces and addictions are a result of "I-making" patterns in our conditioning. Almost everyone faces this dilemma when we go on a meditation retreat. We are forced to let go of our habit patterns by the demands of the schedule. You eat at a specified time and not when you wish to; you wake up when the bell rings and not when you wish to. You are forced to give up your own sense of how things should be in order to honor the boundaries set up for everyone's comfort and well-being.

Then something funny happens. You find out that letting go of your preference for or addiction to your habits is not such a big deal. You adapt rather easily to the new situation and the new structure; you find that once your resistance to new ways of doing things is gone, you even begin to enjoy yourself within the integrity of the schedule.

The lesson here is that we can transport this built-in adaptability to our daily lives. All creatures, including humans, are quite good at adapting to a new environment. When forced to, we adapt to living with a minimum of comfort and greater attention to what's going on around us.

We can reprogram our *ideas* about sickness, aging, and dying and open up to a new landscape in which these processes are seen for what they are: natural events taking place according to causes and conditions. In this new landscape, there is no need to feel incomplete in the face of these natural events. The radical idea of the Buddha in this mix was to suggest, as well as demonstrate, that the self-discipline of the eightfold path brings an end to the perpetual sense of incompletion. Letting go of the sense of incompletion may give us a taste of *nibbāna*, the peace that passeth understanding: the quenching of thirst without material possessions or being addicted to physical comfort or preferences for likes or dislikes.

That simple idea still remains operative. We can discipline our habit forces, our likes and dislikes, our preferences for this or that, and yet let all the six hungry creatures find that balance where things are seen and appreciated for what they are—without giving in to the pleasure or displeasure of consumption of them.

Reflections: Gloria Taraniya Ambrosia

The pull of the six senses is strong. Or, better said, our habit of attaching to what arises at the six sense doors is so strong that it often overtakes us. From one moment to the next our attention is hijacked by what is happening—what we see, hear, smell, taste, touch, and think/feel. We become preoccupied with experience at these levels. What we know from our practice is that the unguarded mind proliferates about sensory contact ... and that heedless proliferation is a set-up for habitual states of mind, many of which are the various forms of longing and resistance that constitute our suffering. This sutta reminds us that in order to offset the habit of mindlessly following impulses, we need to be settled in the direct experience of the body. Grounded. Present.

Many years ago I began taking note of my state of mind in the first moments of wakefulness each day. As I lie in bed, I notice the flood of sensory experience—the array of sensations, feelings, and thoughts that immediately vie for my attention. I watch as the mind habitually seeks refuge in proliferation—deluding itself into believing that there are problems in my life, and that these need to be addressed ... right now! I've noticed that some of this early-morning chatter contains nasty critiques regarding yesterday's actions and inactions … followed by promises to do better. Some of it involves plans and agendas—directives as to what I need to do and who I need to become. Sometimes the mind simply drifts, re-establishing itself in bygone entertainments or dreams.

Watching over the years … it hasn't taken long for me to grow sick of the whole mess, sick of being drawn in. I determined to pump up the volume on mindfulness of the body, to refrain from getting out of bed until I am confident that I have relinquished my grip on the proliferation and become fully established in the body. "I won't get up," I tell myself, "until I'm actually here in the body."

Often just the reminder brings me back. But many mornings the mind seems determined to whine and complain about this ache or pain, that issue or concern, and I can only just barely resist. Some mornings there is such a cloud in the mind that I can only vaguely see. But I really work at it, and over the years my mornings are growing infinitely more settled and peaceful. The Buddha was right. Like the six animals, the mind actually becomes interested in staying put and being present. It's lovely.

To be honest, I have to admit that some of this presence of mind is just one more of the blessings of old age. I no longer have the energy to pick up on my own internal chatter! But most of it proceeds from an ever-growing capacity to stand clear of proliferation and to anchor the six senses by connecting with the body. As practitioners, we want to reflect back to ourselves how good it feels to be HERE and to be anchored in this way.

7.3 Working with Fear

Before my enlightenment,
while I was still only an unenlightened Bodhisatta,
I considered thus:
'Remote jungle-thicket resting places in the forest
are hard to endure ...
the jungles must rob a bhikkhu of his mind,
if he has no concentration.'

I considered thus:
'Whenever recluses or brahmins
    unpurified in bodily conduct ...
    unpurified in verbal conduct ...
    unpurified in mental conduct ...
    unpurified in livelihood ...
resort to remote jungle-thicket resting places in the forest,
then owing to the defect of their unpurified [bodily] conduct
these good recluses and brahmins evoke unwholesome fear
and dread.

But I do not resort to remote jungle-thicket resting places in
the forest
unpurified in [bodily] conduct.
I am purified in [bodily] conduct.
I resort to remote jungle-thicket resting places in the forest
as one of the noble ones with [bodily] conduct purified.'
Seeing in myself this purity of [bodily] conduct,
I found great solace in dwelling in the forest.

I considered thus:
'There are the specially auspicious nights
of the fourteenth, the fifteenth, and the eighth of the
fortnight.
Now what if, on such nights as these,
I were to dwell in such awe-inspiring, horrifying abodes
as orchard shrines, woodland shrines, and tree shrines?

188 • Older and Wiser

Perhaps I might encounter that fear and dread.'

And later, on such specially auspicious nights
    as the fourteenth, the fifteenth, and the eighth of the
fortnight,
    I dwelt in such awe-inspiring, horrifying abodes
    as orchard shrines, woodland shrines, and tree shrines.

And while I dwelt there,
a wild animal would come up to me,
or a peacock would knock off a branch,
or the wind would rustle the leaves.

I thought: 'What now if this is the fear and dread coming?'
I thought: 'Why do I dwell always expecting fear and dread?
What if I subdue that fear and dread
while keeping the same posture
that I am in when it comes upon me?'

While I walked, the fear and dread came upon me;
I neither stood nor sat nor lay down
till I had subdued that fear and dread.

While I stood, the fear and dread came upon me;
I neither walked nor sat nor lay down
till I had subdued that fear and dread.

While I sat, the fear and dread came upon me;
I neither walked nor stood nor lay down
till I had subdued that fear and dread.

While I lay down, the fear and dread came upon me;
I neither walked nor stood nor sat down
till I had subdued that fear and dread.

(Bhayabherava Sutta, Majjhima Nikāya 4)

Reflections: Andrew Olendzki

Many have remarked how unusual it is that we do not hear much about fear in early Buddhist teachings, given how central a phenomenon it is in Western psychology. It seems to be regarded as a manifestation of aversion, where we might see things the other way around (aversion being rooted in fear). This text is one exception, a rare instance in which the Buddha speaks directly to the matter of fear by citing his own struggles with it before his enlightenment (after which all fear is put to rest, of course). Several things jump out at us here:

1) He seems to be making a direct link between the arising of fear and one's own ethical conduct, suggesting that fear will only come up to afflict those who are 'unpurified' in thought, word, and deed. This sounds unusual to our modern ear. It might have to do with a notion that the demons who inhabit such fearful places will especially punish the wicked with their afflictions. Or perhaps it comes from a sense that one can only misbehave by suppressing the conscience (*hiri*) and respect (*ottappa*) that are inherent in the mind, and thus guilt and shame may be a source of fear. Certainly the Buddhist tradition encourages ethical conduct in part as a protection against fear, and suggests that if we have not misbehaved generally we generally have nothing to fear.

2) The Buddha deliberately puts himself in a position to experience fear. It is as if he were working with it as a practice, conjuring up the fear just so he could overcome it. This seems a bit like modern exposure therapy, wherein one eventually gets over one's phobias by a gradual exposure to them in a safe setting. This shows courage on the Buddha's part, as well as commitment.

3) Despite the phrase 'I subdued that fear,' I get a sense that the Buddha's main strategy here is to allow the experience of fear to arise and pass away naturally—hence not moving until it has passed. We know that giving in to the fear will only make it stronger, but trying to suppress or deny the fear is an aversive response that will also strengthen its power. The middle ground between these two approaches is to be aware of it as it arises, as it persists, and as it passes away, as it inevitably will do if we do not feed it by either welcoming or rejecting it.

Placing this teaching in the context of retirement, we recognize that aging, illness, and dying are all possible triggers of fear. If we wish, we can choose to follow the Buddha's lead

190 • Older and Wiser

by facing up to these fears rather than trying to avoid them. It is just another emotion, just another phenomenon of experience, just another event to be investigated that will arise and pass away from time to time. It causes suffering in us to the extent that we focus on the content of our fears—"what might happen?" —but diminishes when we are able to focus instead on the process— arising, persisting, passing away. Let it come. Let it go.

Reflections: Mu Soeng

What comes to mind upon first reading this poem is the issue of Primal Fear. The Buddha seems to be saying that he went to extremes in order to confront this primal fear—the death instinct. The Buddha also seems to be saying that he had to go through this process in order to break through to an awareness that is not conditioned by the death instinct. I think this idea needs some careful unpacking.

The liberation project of the Buddha seems to focus on two aspects: the psychological and the instinctual. Although there invariably are overlaps between these two aspects, the psychological may be described as the ego-based functioning of the conditioned personality. An ego is a construct—familial, social, cultural, and so on. The instinctual, on the other hand, is biological and operates on the demands of comfort and survival. In this way, the biological is more primary than the ego function.

We can perhaps see these layers in our experiences of sickness, aging, and dying. If we look carefully, we might find that our primary concerns with respect to these experiences are biological—making the body more comfortable, making it less painful, or making it totally pain-free. The ego, meanwhile, continues to intrude and create scenarios of what it would be like when the body is totally pain-free, what "I" would be able to do, to accomplish, and so on.

The testimony of the Buddha is that he consciously confronted these primal fears of biological extinction by putting himself in those dangerous situations in the forest, and thereby was able to overcome the habitual ego-constructs. If the basic problem confronted in the liberation project of the Buddha is the working of greed, hatred, and delusion, it would seem logical to suppose that these are workings of ego-construct and do not define the total personality. The totality of the human being (or beings of any species, for that matter) is the biological, and to confront the fear of biological extinction (which, incidentally, seems unique to human beings) is the primary task of the liberation project.

If this premise is correct, we can investigate our experiences of sickness, aging, and dying more closely and see that there are stories about these experiences, and there are the experiences themselves. The experiences themselves are changing moment by moment, but the stories may remain fixated. Allowing our experiences to unfold naturally in each moment may be a way to confront the primal fear in a way similar to that employed by the Buddha.

Reflections: Gloria Taraniya Ambrosia

In many of the suttas in the Pāli Canon, the Buddha generously shares intimate accounts of his own practice. I find these accounts very helpful. It's as if he takes us by the hand and guides us: "This is how you free the mind." The current sutta is a good example. Here, a Brahmin asks about the difficulty of practicing in remote jungle thickets. People left alone in scary places can go mad, he says, especially if their concentration is not well developed. The Buddha agrees ... and proceeds to tell a practice story that took place before his enlightenment.

With the intention of encountering and conquering fear and dread, he entered the scariest parts of the forest—such "horrifying abodes as orchard shrines, woodland shrines, and tree shrines." It was a common belief of the time that demons infested the forest on observance (*uposatha*) days and captured those who were not spiritually endowed. Practicing in the forest on these days would have been tantamount to going to a haunted house on Halloween!

If we follow his process, we see that the Buddha noticed what was happening and then noticed his reaction. At first a "wild animal would come upon him, or a peacock would knock a branch of a tree, or the wind would rustle the leaves" ... and then he felt fear and dread. But rather than getting caught up in these, he stood his ground until the fear and dread subsided. As he put it, if he was standing, he continued to stand, if he was sitting, he continued to sit, and so forth.

There are several important messages in this teaching. The wisdom path involves courage and determination. One must knuckle down and face what arises ... resisting the temptation to turn to the old ways to cope with difficult arisings. The highly conditioned tendency is to get lost in fear, to run away, or to ignore it. But this sutta demonstrates the importance of meeting things head on. We know from our own practice, for example, that one of the chief obstacles to realizing insight into *dukkha* is constantly changing postures in response to moments of discomfort. And here we have the Buddha demonstrating the importance of staying with what is happening ... keeping the mind steady and open.

The sutta also points to the link between facing our most primitive fears and liberating the mind. No longer bound by the old ways, we stop protecting a sense of self that isn't real and doesn't need defending. Thus we break deeply entrenched patterns of delusion.

Finally, this story shows the correlation between purity and a sense of ease and focus. The Buddha found great solace in dwelling in the forest—largely because he was pure in bodily, verbal, and mental conduct, free of the hindrances, not given to self-aggrandizement, not swayed by the worldly dhammas. His mind was energetic, mindful, and concentrated. He enjoyed dwelling in forest groves because doing so provides a pleasant abiding here and now and contributes to the good of all beings.

7.4 Living in Harmony

On one occasion the bhikkhus at Kosambi
had taken to quarreling and brawling
and were deep in disputes,
stabbing each other with verbal daggers.

They could neither convince each other
nor be convinced by others;
they could neither persuade each other
nor be persuaded by others.

Then the Buddha
addressed a certain bhikkhu thus:
Come, bhikkhu, tell those bhikkhus in my name
that the Teacher calls them.

"Yes, venerable sir," he replied,
and he went to those bhikkhus and told them:
"The Teacher calls the venerable ones."

"Yes, friend," they replied,
and they went to the Blessed One,
and after paying homage to him,
they sat down at one side.

The Buddha then asked them:

Bhikkhus, what do you think?
When you take to quarreling and brawling
and are deep in disputes,
stabbing each other with verbal daggers,
do you on that occasion
maintain acts of loving-kindness
by body, speech, and mind
in public and in private
towards your companions in the holy life?

"No, venerable sir."

What can you possibly know, what can you see,
that you take to quarreling and brawling
and are deep in disputes,
stabbing each other with verbal daggers?
That you can neither convince each other
nor be convinced by others,
that you can neither persuade each other
nor be persuaded by others?

That will lead to your harm and suffering for a long time.

Then the Buddha addressed the bhikkhus thus:

Bhikkhus, there are these six principles of cordiality
that create love and respect
and conduce to cohesion, to non-dispute,
to concord, and to unity.
What are the six?

1. Here a bhikkhu maintains
   bodily acts of loving-kindness
   both in public and in private
   towards his companions in the holy life.

2. Again, a bhikkhu maintains
   verbal acts of loving-kindness
   both in public and in private
   towards his companions in the holy life.

3. Again, a bhikkhu maintains
   mental acts of loving-kindness
   both in public and in private
   towards his companions in the holy life.

4. Again, a bhikkhu uses things in common
   with his virtuous companions in the holy life;
   without making reservations,
   he shares with them any gain of a kind
   that accords with the Dhamma
   and has been obtained in a way
   that accords with the Dhamma,
   including even the mere contents of his bowl.

5. Again, a bhikkhu dwells
   both in public and in private
   possessing in common
   with his companions in the holy life
   those virtues that are unbroken, untorn,
   unblotched, unmottled, liberating,
   commended by the wise,
   not misapprehended,
   and conducive to concentration.

6. Again, a bhikkhu dwells
   both in public and in private
   possessing in common with his companions in the holy life
   that view that is noble and emancipating,
   and leads one who practices in accordance with it
   to the complete destruction of suffering.

These are the six principles of cordiality
that create love and respect,
and conduce to cohesion, to non-dispute,
to concord, and to unity.

(Kosambiya Sutta, Majjhima Nikāya 48)

Reflections: Andrew Olendzki

Getting along with others in a harmonious way is a theme for any age and any stage of life. I love this metaphor of "stabbing each other with verbal daggers." This is so much what it feels like when we argue with one another, isn't it?

But the most provocative passage is the Buddha's challenge, "What can you possibly know, what can you see, that you take to quarreling …" In other words, what is so compelling that it takes a higher priority than getting along with one another? He says this in the context of the monastic community, but surely it applies as well to our families, our partnerships, our work environments, and—why not? —perhaps even our nations.

196 • Older and Wiser

When in conflict, it is easy to lose the larger perspective and grasp tightly to our views and opinions, our preferences, and our beliefs. Is being right or winning the argument really more important than the wellbeing of all? There may be some situations in which a great deal is at stake, but most of our quarrels fall well below this threshold, and most of the wounds we inflict with our words are not warranted.

The Buddha goes on to expound a set of general principles that are conducive to harmony among people, and I think much of Buddhist practice has to do with manifesting these principles in our everyday life. Most Buddhists (both today and throughout history) are not meditators, but do share a commitment to acting with as much integrity as possible in their lives.

The first three of these principles is quite straightforward: maintain an attitude of loving-kindness in all you think, say, and do. It sounds so simple, and yet is very hard to accomplish. It requires a diligence that can only come from mindfulness—an internal emotional diligence. Whatever attitude or emotion is in one's mind will shape what is thought, said, and done. One is not capable of wounding another with mental, verbal, or physical daggers if an attitude of loving-kindness is maintained. And without this kindness, we are capable of inflicting any level of harm.

The fourth principle, sharing, involves a mind-state rooted in generosity. When we give something to another we are relinquishing our hold on it and offering it for the benefit of the other. A moment of sharing is a moment of caring more about someone else than about oneself. It is relatively easy to give an object to another, but what about conceding a point in an argument? This too can be seen as an expression of generosity.

The last two principles are very wide in scope, encompassing all the Buddhist virtues and the broad notion of right view. These have to do with cultivating mind-states that are rooted in generosity, kindness, and wisdom rather than those rooted in greed, hatred, and delusion. Unwholesome states separate and divide; wholesome states unify and mend—it's as simple as that. What can we all possibly know and see that renders it more important to hurt one another than to help make one another be happy and well?

Reflections: Mu Soeng

What I appreciate here is the emphasis on the value of cultivating mind-states rooted in generosity, kindness, and wisdom that can provide an anchor in our own internal dialogue where we often torture ourselves with regrets and projections. As a way of describing the working of the internal dialogue, T.S. Eliot famously wrote: "And I pray that I may forget/ These matters that with myself I too much discuss/ Too much explain."

While the Buddha speaks of verbal daggers thrown at others in interpersonal relationships, perhaps the greater task is to stop sharpening those daggers in our own conditioning processes. In our internal dialogues we can, and often do, quite easily throw verbal daggers and pick up various quarrels with ourselves. The verbal daggers we throw and various quarrels we pick are more often a reflection of our own internal dialogues. The Buddha's suggestion for cultivating loving-kindness as a way of ending these quarrels and verbal daggers is just as much an antidote for our own internal dialogue, where we accept ourselves as our best friend.

To accept ourselves as our best friend, we must pass through the eye of the needle: the quenching of thirsts of all kinds. Seeing the pettiness and shallowness of our own internal dialogues is a good way to investigate how our quarrels with ourselves and with others are shallow and petty. What is to be gained? In our disputes with others, we project a certain knowing that we feel is superior to others' knowing, but close examination reveals that all we know is so porous that it is hardly reliable. Most of all, we don't even know ourselves. Our ideas are merely conjectures, not the universally valid principles we sometimes take them to be.

We can learn to have compassion for our conditioned existence. All human beings are conflicted to some extent, some more than others. It is the basic *dukkha* of human existence. The

Buddha taught the practice of loving-kindness as an antidote to conflict, both within and with others. It brings a stabilizing peacefulness that allows us to probe deeply into our conditioned existence without being destabilized by what we find in there. It opens up a space that then allows us to live in cordiality with both others and ourselves.

Reflections: Gloria Taraniya Ambrosia

One of the things that comes up most often in Dhamma discussions with mature practitioners is how surprised they are at the vitality of their quarrelsome natures. Even after many years of practice, the mind seems determined to find fault with self and others ... and at times this fault-finding can occupy much of our internal energy. Sometimes the mind just goes on and on about nothing, and we can feel helpless (hopeless!) in our ability to make it stop. One could say, "Well, just stop thinking those thoughts," but it's not that easy, is it? The unawakened mind is strongly habituated to quarreling.

Interestingly, the quarrel at Kosambi grew out of a misunderstanding regarding an insignificant transgression of a minor rule ... but in no time at all the battle sides were drawn, factions established, and a full-blown schism at hand. Perhaps we can take a twisted comfort in knowing that even the *sangha*, with their sophisticated training rules and high renunciation, couldn't stop the flood of adversity. Even the wise counsel of the Buddha couldn't turn their habits and confusion around! How much more might we be helpless in the face of quarrelsome impulses?

As the years go by, as we age and approach nearer to death, one can feel the urgency to STOP ARGUING—both internally and externally. In his teachings, the Buddha often emphasized the importance of restraining or turning the attention elsewhere to offset unskillful habits. These are very important strategies. In this sutta, however, he focuses on the development side of the equation—encouraging the cultivation of kindness, generosity, calm, and insight. These qualities are key players in the process of waking up. They establish a softness in the mind that both offsets our habit of buying into quarrelsome thinking and ultimately makes it possible to uproot that kind of thinking altogether. Here the Buddha encourages us to be kind through body, speech, and mind. Be generous, willing to share what we have learned, what we have acquired. Behave in ways that are conducive to calm, that give us a leg up on stillness. All of these bring about a quietude that helps diminish the tendency to quarrel. Finally, the Buddha encourages us to sort out the confusion of the mind by seeing clearly.

This last point might be the most difficult. The Buddha encourages us to develop right view— "that which leads to the complete destruction of suffering." Right view makes it possible for us to see thought as thought, to know the pain of being preoccupied with harmful and contentious thought, to know the sense of self that lies at the heart of our grasping, and to become adept at the wise attention that makes it possible to stop feeding foolishness. It's pretty basic stuff ... but it is years in the unfolding.

In the end, it's not the conditions of life that create our suffering; it's our persistent delusion about what constitutes an efficacious response. Quarreling is never a suitable response. It only gets us deeper in. We need to see what the mind is doing and learn to relate to it with some semblance of objectivity.

Suggested Questions for Study Groups

A Shift in Focus

1.1   Bhaddiya Gets Free

Reflection #1: Andrew compares the relief Bhaddiya felt living the homeless life of a monk to what we might experience as we move into our senior years. One is relieved of some of burdens of youth and the responsibilities of family and employment. One is freer to pursue spiritual goals. One might say all that remains is to recognize this opportunity and use it well. Still, there is a momentum to being occupied and preoccupied with the things of the world. And it can be difficult to turn that momentum around.

Are you finding that you are able to use the opportunity that aging affords to turn towards spiritual goals? If you are having difficulty shifting gears, can you identify what those difficulties are and determine how to work with them?

Reflection #2: Bhaddiya's experience is somewhat unique in that he was high born and thus may have enjoyed greater creature comforts, power, and influence than many of us. Still, perhaps we can relate to the feeling of fear and anxiety he experienced lest these be lost or challenged. We pay a high price for building up our treasures in the world and attaching to them.

This sutta points to the downside to having it all. Objects tend to own us, instead of the other way around. Are you glad for the release from responsibilities—even if only partial? What has been your experience? Take some time to reflect upon this and talk about it with your dhamma friends.

Reflection #3: Generally speaking, one might say that the Buddhist teachings and practices turn things a bit upside down. In our youth we might believe that consuming and accumulating things, gratifying ourselves through the world is the path to

202 • Older and Wiser

happiness. And we may have enjoyed relative happiness in that enterprise. But as we age, and with the help of the insights we garner through Buddhist teachings and practices, we begin to see through the premise that happiness is found in worldly objects. We examine the relationship between accumulation and contentment, between having and being. Thus, we are freer to relate to the world with less attachment.

Are you finding this to be true? Take some time to reflect upon this and talk about it with your dhamma friends.

1.2   Ten Things to Reflect Upon

Reflection #1: On first glance, these ten reflections may strike one as intense and even harsh. Clearly, these constitute a no-nonsense evaluation of one's actions through body, speech, and mind—an evaluation that one would be wise to consider daily.

You might want to take up these ten reflections for a period of time and notice the impact on your daily life. See if you agree with Mu Soeng when he says, "If we adopt the ten things mentioned in this text as a way to prepare for all eventualities, our passage through our elder years might be so much more harmonious." He notes that whether we prepare for them or not, life's eventualities may be forced on us anyway, so one might say that it is better to be prepared.

Reflection #2: Mu Soeng draws a parallel between our "going forth" into retirement years and the processes of aging and death, with someone going forth from a householder's life to a homeless life in the Buddha's community. "Both," he says, "embark upon new training steps (*sikha padam*) to embrace a new phase in life for which there are few guidelines but plenty of lessons to be learned." Gloria Taraniya draws similar parallels in the previous section (See *1.1: Bhaddiya Gets Free*).

Do you agree with these parallels? Do you have any examples or stories you can offer in a discussion with your dhamma friends?

Reflection #3: Gloria Taraniya points to the value of the fourth recollection— "Do I reproach myself in regard to virtuous behavior?" She makes an interesting distinction between the usefulness of remorse and the agitation caused by regret. The latter, she says, has more to do with the mental hindrance of restlessness and worry, and it serves no useful purpose. But remorse is a manifestation of *hiri* and *ottappa,* which together are the ability to differentiate between what is worthy of respect and what is not. They are called the guardians of the universe, and one can see why.

As you practice, see if you can notice the distinction in your mind and heart between useful reflection on your actions and reflection that pulls you down into regret. Do you see what Gloria Taraniya is pointing to here? Do you find this distinction useful?

1.3   Higher Pleasures

Reflection #1: Andrew writes in his essay that, "The pleasure of not having and not needing to have is more subtle than that of sensual gratification." He also notes, however, that the Buddha clearly states that this is not a lesser pleasure. In fact, it is a far greater one! This point is worthy of contemplation and observation. Can we verify that a greater pleasure comes from not wanting or needing an object in the first place? This greater pleasure is not just feeling the delight of letting go ... it is an organic pleasure that comes from having uprooted craving.

As you age and mature, are you able to take a dispassionate look at the totality of your life's experience? And can you feel the subtle difference between these two? What are your thoughts or comments? Have you some examples or stories you can offer in a discussion with your dhamma friends?

Reflection #2: It seems to me that this sutta passage opens up an interesting distance between the categories of gratification and enjoyment. The Buddha seems to be saying that seeking gratification in sensual pleasures is a "lower pleasure" because the conclusion does not bring about a sense of fulfillment. On

204 • Older and Wiser

the other hand, according to the Buddha, the practice of non-grasping leads to a "higher pleasure." In this respect, calling it a higher pleasure creates an interesting *koan*.

How does it work out in your own life experience? Is it a sense of fulfillment? A sense of closure? A sense of resolution? Something else?

Reflection #3: Gloria Taraniya's reflection points to an organic maturation process that takes place over the years of our lives. In our youth, we quite naturally seek happiness in worldly pursuits, and we enjoy some happiness there. But over the years, it is not at all uncommon for each and every one of us to realize the transient nature of sensual pleasures and to look for a less superficial peace.

The Buddha said that by seeing sense pleasures as they actually are—seeing their origin, disappearance, gratification, danger and escape—he went beyond superficial happiness and arrived at profound peace of mind. Our task as practitioners is to walk through these same five realizations—however subtly or profoundly we might go about that—and allow these truths to sink in. This is our path, our investigation, our letting go. As your practice matures … are you seeing this for yourself? Write about it. Talk about it with your dhamma friends.

1.4   Looking Forward to Retirement

Reflection #1: Mu Soeng refers again to the ashrama model in ancient India wherein both husband and wife might retire to a spiritual community in their "golden years" and use it as their metaphorical cave to be protected from the stress of the householder's life they have lived with all their lives. He says that it is possible for any serious practitioner to repurpose and rearrange his or her life according to the principles of living simply and dying joyfully, even while working tirelessly to uproot greed, hatred, and delusion.

Can you re-imagine your retirement years in this way by committing yourself more fully to the training in *sīla, samādhi,* and *paññā*? Can you imagine this training process as a deeper internalization of these factors? How does it sound as a "vision" for retirement years, and how do you see the ease or difficulty of translating this vision into reality?

Reflection #2: Gloria Taraniya says in her reflections that as the physical energy level declines in our golden years, "the wisdom factor has matured to a point where it is actually possible to clearly see the machinations of self-concern for what they are—fabrications of a mind that has probably spent lifetimes in delusion."

To what extent are you able to connect with this observation? What are the consequences for this clarity in our emotional and psychological lives?

Reflection #3: Andrew comments that "desire is the very thing that complexifies any life, as one wish after another rises up to demand satisfaction and we hustle endlessly to assuage them all." Most likely, we all know this feeling. And we, like Tālaputa, long for a time when greed and hatred are finally put to rest and we can enjoy peace of mind. We imagine ourselves "seated in bliss, despite the many challenges of aging."

Have you imagined yourself so? Or imagined yourself in some state that at least approaches such freedom? Do you ever find that this kind of aspiration can stand in the way of actually realizing it? Describe your experience.

Equanimity

2.1   Beyond Joy and Sorrow

Reflection #1: If we are honest we'll admit that in our youth we were accustomed to spending significant amounts of time and energy trying to create conditions that we hoped would bring about desirable pleasant results. As a strategy for happiness, this may have felt sensible and reasonable. We may have been disappointed more than once, but we probably kept it

206 • Older and Wiser

up for some time. As we mature, however, we see the downside of wanting and not-wanting, of expectation and manipulation. We learn that if our contentment depends upon receiving the things that will delight us, or avoiding what causes distress, it will remain shallow.

Contemplate this matter; reflect upon it. Can you relate? Do you find these observations to be true for you? Can you describe the process whereby you facilitated or simply witnessed an internal shift in that wanting and not wanting? What was it like before? What is it like now? You might find it helpful to express your thoughts in writing or to discuss them with a dhamma friend.

Reflection #2: With this teaching, we seem to be talking about both contentment and equanimity. In the Buddhist teachings, the word contentment often refers to one's capacity to be content with "any robe or bowl," to be content with whatever one is offered. The idea is to not want more, not begrudge less. The word equanimity points to an even-mindedness in the face of every sort of experience, regardless of whether it's painful or pleasant. Equanimity is born out of wisdom—that is, having seen for ourselves "that longing and resisting don't bring about the desired results," as Gloria Taraniya puts it.

As you reflect upon this sutta, are you aware of the ways in which contentment and equanimity are similar experiences? Are you aware of the ways in which they are different? Contemplate this for yourself. It is very important that we "recognize and acknowledge the little ways that we are getting free," notes Gloria Taraniya. You might find it helpful to express your thoughts in writing or to discuss them with a dhamma friend.

Reflection #3: In the unawakened state, our entire human experience is shaped by the desire to be and the desire to have. As Mu Soeng puts it, quenching these fires is our "unfinished business." Our practice is directed toward going beyond [seeking] delight and [avoiding] distress and realizing the Middle Way. Bhikkhu Bodhi describes this mind-state as a "a mind that has become pliable; become stable; become flexible; reached a state of not fluttering." Andrew notes that conventional thinking often describes this middle emotional range "as boring or bland," but that those who have experienced it firsthand know better.

Have you had glimpses into this "non-fluttering" state? Contemplate your experience and discuss it with your dhamma friends. Elaborate on your experience so as to make it more fully conscious.

Reflection #4: As Andrew writes: "Any time we want things to be different than they are, we are setting ourselves up for disappointment. This is because delight and distress are two sides of the same coin, and we cannot have one without the other. It is precisely because he is not consumed with delight that the Buddha can 'sit alone, without being consumed by regret.'"

What is it like to live without being consumed by delight or regret? Have you known this state of peaceful equanimity, contentment rooted in wisdom—even if only for a few moments? Take some time and recollect that state and know that it is possible.

2.2 Sleeping Well

Reflection #1: Andrew goes to the heart of the problem with these reflections: "What use are all the worldly blessings, not only of a comfortable bed but also of youth, health, prestige, and wealth, if one's mind is not settled and roils with afflicted emotions? ... The stabbing arrow of always wanting and needing more, no matter what one already has acquired ... cause far more distress in the night than a lumpy bed."

What is your own experience with this kind of dynamic? Perhaps one enjoys a high degree of physical comfort but then has to deal with the stresses and pressures of protecting these and/or acquiring more. Thus, we are both comforted and stressed by the same things. Perhaps there is physical comfort, but the mind is tormented with worldly concerns. Have you seen this? How do you balance this tension? How do you find peace within the complexities of a Western householder's life?

208 • Older and Wiser

Reflection #2: In this poem, the Buddha defines "resting at ease in every way" as a result of burning off the fires of greed, hatred, and delusion. While we may not have extinguished these flames entirely ... no doubt we have all had glimpses into the experience of release. Can you recall moments when you felt completely at ease with what was happening, with yourself or with others? Can you outline the ingredients of those moments when the fires of greed, hatred, and delusion were held at bay? Give some thought to how you cultivate those ingredients in an ongoing manner.

Reflection #3: Both Gloria Taraniya and Mu Soeng point to the importance of insight into the nature of things as the way to offset the fires of greed, hatred, and delusion. Mu Soeng points to a Zen teaching that encourages us to accept things as they are by witnessing the tension between the direct experience of phenomena (which is inherently neutral) and our evaluation of it as either good and bad (which is a fabrication of the mind). When we dwell in the true nature of things, we enjoy contentment and ease of being. Things are the way they are. We accept that and release the tension born of ignorance.

Gloria Taraniya notes that awakening is "a gradual and sometimes brutally slow process of experiencing for ourselves both the harm and pain of these three unwholesome roots of suffering ... and the great happiness and benefit of their wholesome opposites." This transformation proceeds from the direct experience of suffering and its release through practice, and it results in the very happy experience of a heart that is no longer troubled by unwholesome impulses or actions through body, speech, or mind—a heart that has realized right view and right thought.

As you explore and experience what it means to be fully at ease with yourself and with the conditions of your life—to accept things as they are—how would you describe your overall contentment? And how does this manifest in the quality of your sleep?

2.3 The Single Most Precious Moment

Reflection #1: In this sutta the Buddha encourages us to let go of the past and cease worrying about the future. Alternatively, he encourages us to turn to that which is before us in the present moment and garner insight through that focus. But how? How does one do that? The Buddha both asks and answers the question: How does one not chase after what is gone? And how does one not yearn for what is yet to be? Examining his answer, we realize that the method, if you will, is non-attachment to the body and mind, that is, to the five aggregates.

That's a big job. But as Gloria Taraniya notes: "While some might say that as we age our attachments become more entrenched through years of repetition and delusion ... for serious practitioners who are paying attention even just a little, there is also the very real possibility of learning to stand back from it all, to see body, feeling, perception, formations, and consciousness without identification."

As your practice matures, and as you cultivate non-attachment to the body and mind, have you found yourself becoming more entrenched – OR – resting more fully in the present moment? Consider precise examples of this. Reflect upon how it feels to be entrenched in attachment and how it feels to be free of it. Be on the lookout for such moments each day so that your realizations can deepen.

Reflection #2: It is incumbent upon all practitioners to see for ourselves how the sense of self is formed and crystalized around attachment to the five aggregates. Mu Soeng helps this insight along by offering an interesting distinction between functional thinking versus self-oriented thinking about the future. "If your roof is leaking," he says, "you need to arrange for a roofer to come and fix it. This planning about the future is purely functional. It does not involve thinking about the self or its past or its future. On the other hand, constantly recreating a self in the events of the past or possibilities of the future is purely a speculative engagement, and an unwholesome one."

210 • Older and Wiser

Have you seen the difference between such functional thinking and the kind of thinking that generates and strengthens a sense of self? Can you offer examples? What is the direct experience of being caught up in either mode—that is, how does it feel? Do you find this thoughtful distinction useful as you endeavor to see attachment to the body and mind and the effect it has?

Reflection #3: Andrew notes that the fruit of examining the present moment in ways that are not bound up with the construction of self is the experience of "a single most precious moment." Gloria Taraniya notes that release from self-absorbed thinking and attachment, which is the principle cause of our suffering, is no less than the realization of *nibbāna*, the highest happiness.

It is not uncommon for practitioners to think of such precious moments, of *nibbāna,* as a remote or inaccessible experience. Considering these passages, however, we might realize that perhaps present moment existence is far more accessible than we imagine. Yes, we may only get glimpses in our daily practice, but those glimpses can fuel our practice for many years.

What is your experience of present moment reality? Even if you've only had glimpses, how have they affected your practice and your understanding?

2.4   Two Ways to Prepare

Reflection #1: Andrew says that it makes sense to prepare for the possibility of diminished health and many other forms of loss as we age. We do this to enjoy a certain freedom in our old age. But, he writes, the Buddha encourages us to think about old age in a different way and suggests that we would be better off "unburdening rather than accumulating, relinquishing rather than holding on, opening up to the radical contingency of our situation with trust and peace rather than trying to hold off and resist what we know deep down to be inevitable." This kind of approach, Andrew writes, points to a "higher freedom" that is not dependent on possessions and resources.

What are your thoughts on this? Does the phrase "higher freedom" make sense in today's world, especially as we negotiate our entanglements with possessions and resources and pressures of aging and sickness? Can you imagine or have you experienced a decidedly greater freedom through gradually diminishing dependence on possessions?

<u>Reflection #2</u>: All of the authors reiterate the Buddha's encouragement to realize the importance of a well-trained mind and to develop it. Andrew points to the reliability of a well-ordered mind over reliance on resources. Mu Soeng notes, "A well-trained mind can guide us to the awareness "that aging and sickness are an integral part of the ecosystem of the body, and we can make peace with them." Gloria Taraniya notes that while it is important to provide for our worldly health, none of those preparations guarantee our ultimate welfare or our liberation before we die. As a way of evaluating our development, she encourages an internal examination by asking a series of questions:

"How's our capacity to see the hindrances as they arise and to get a handle on these?

"Do we see the longing and resistance in the heart?

"Have we subdued the floods of *kilesā*, the fires of desire, the fetter of attachment?

"Is the mind tight or too loose? Stubborn or malleable? Contracted and bound or kind and non-judgmental?

"Maybe our worldly affairs are in order, but do we clearly see that *anicca, dukkha* and *anattā* still rule the day?"

Perhaps you would like to take some time and do an internal weather report with these questions as your guide. What is your experience of making peace with conditions through developing your mind? Do you have a sense of it as a home, a refuge, a container, a protection, an embrace, especially as you confront old age and prospective death?

212 • Older and Wiser

Reflection #3: Gloria Taraniya points to the different experience of householders compared to nuns and monks. As householders and Buddhist practitioners, we have to juggle both worldly and unworldly objectives. It's incumbent on us to eke out a lifestyle based in the world, but which also supports relating appropriately to that world—that is, without attachment. It's up to us to determine how to live within the complexities of Western culture and at the same time stride towards freedom.

How do you reconcile the need to navigate the complexities of living in a complex culture with your aspiration to settle the mind enough to see clearly? Are they mutually exclusive? Is liberation as a householder impossible or entirely too difficult? Or do you agree with Gloria Taraniya that it is possible to get our worldly affairs in order such that in our senior years we are freer to practice for liberation with greater interest and enthusiasm than ever before?

AGING

3.1   The Lucidity of Age

Reflection #1: We have all seen the physical changes that come with age—weakness of muscles, declining energy, hair falling out, bones becoming brittle. We usually assume a certain amount of mental decline as well, but does that necessarily have to be the case? The Buddha says that he is old, aged, burdened with years, advanced in life—having reached his 80th year. Yet his wisdom is so great that "even if you have to carry me about on a bed, still there will be no change in the lucidity of the Tathāgata's wisdom." This is how clear his wisdom is at the end of his lifespan.

Gloria Taraniya summarizes it this way: "Once we realize that level of wisdom, nothing ... not even a weakened, decrepit, or dying body can take it away. Even sickness, aging, and death are no threat to the liberated mind."

Andrew notes that the mind is not identical with the brain and that current research shows that meditation affects the brain in positive ways. We know how the body affects the mind. Consider, too, how the mind affects the body, that is, how the practice of mindfulness brings positive outcomes.

These ideas might open up new possibilities for many of us. Are these ideas unfathomable? What are your thoughts and observations on this matter? Perhaps you can discuss this with your dhamma friends.

Reflection #2: A natural outcome of right practice is insight into the workings of the mind and the nature of phenomena. "As a result," notes Mu Soeng, "… [one is] somewhat less deluded, so that when delusion arises, there is enough wisdom from earlier cultivation" to stop us in our tracks and start a fresh round of inquiry. He emphasizes this ability to stop delusion in its tracks before spinning out as a hallmark of development.

From your own experience as you age … do you notice that you are able to "return to the refuge" your practice has created and behave more wisely? Has this become a reliable and steady response for you? Please share your thoughts.

Reflection #3: Gloria Taraniya points to a common tendency in our culture to measure a person's worth based on age "with youth assuming the more valued position." She says that it behooves us to give some thought to how we might turn this around: "One isn't advocating a seniors-rights movement," she writes, "… just more clarity internally in our hearts and externally in our communities as to our worth. I think this needs to be acknowledged and addressed because it is hurting us as a society."

What do you think about this? How might we go about changing the values of our society, turning this around? Is that even necessary? Or is it enough that we understand it ourselves, realize our own worth, and behave accordingly?

214 • Older and Wiser

3.2   The Worldly Winds

Reflection #1: As Mu Soeng says, the opening lines of this poem are especially noteworthy: "It is among misfortunes that one's steadfastness is to be known, and this only after a long time, not casually, by one who is attentive, not by one who is inattentive, and by one who is wise, not by one who is unwise." Reading these lines one gets the feeling that there is enough fodder for contemplation to last a lifetime! Steadfastness in the face of adversity reminds us of the *paramis* of determination, patience, balance. The non-casual application of effort, the wise versus unwise attentiveness—all of these evoke images of someone who has done the work of practice and is earning its rewards.

Do these phrases resonate with your practice in daily life? Do you feel that your practice is actively cultivating the equanimity that makes it possible to navigate the worldly winds?

Reflection #2: Gloria Taraniya's story of the interaction with her neighbor is a good example of how insight pops up when we least expect it. In a moment of exasperation, we might let go just enough to stop struggling with the polarities of life and let the truth squeeze through. We struggle with the worldly winds until or unless we learn to settle down beneath appearances into the deeper reality of things. For the moment, the truth sets us free. Lose the clinging to appearances and we lose the anxiety associated with living in the world and becoming a self.

Perhaps you've had similar moments in your life. We can nurture our insights by recollecting them and letting the truth of such moments sink in. This can be a very useful exercise.

Reflection #3: Andrew points to the fact that, given that our lives swing between one end of the pendulum to the other, we are guaranteed to suffer if we do not widen our view to encompass all of it. He says that the Buddha is teaching us here how to roll with things rather than resist them, to adapt, adjust, and accept what happens while retaining a sense of equilibrium. This teaching on the worldly winds is therefore all about maintaining our equilibrium in the presence of the changing tides. We adjust to the inevitable, rather than yearning for the impossible.

It is important to state in our own words the sentiment and wisdom contained in each of the teachings of the Buddha. How would you characterize the primary message of this teaching?

3.3   The Monk and the King

Reflection #1: This sutta points to two levels of insight. As Gloria Taraniya notes ... contemplation of the realities of sickness, aging, and death can bring about a kind of preliminary right view "that is enough to get us going more deliberately on the path towards liberating insight." This, in turn, sets us up for deeper, more penetrating insight. "Gradually ... and over time ... we go beyond opening to sickness, aging, and death and become interested in the deeper truths from which these proceed." This is what Raṭṭhapāla has done. As Andrew notes: "He is pointing toward something more primal than the ordinary conditions of life."

In your own practice, have you seen the difference between these two levels of insight? What are your thoughts regarding these? Please share your actual experiences and realizations.

Reflection #2: As noted in Reflection #1, Raṭṭhapāla encourages the king to go beyond appearances. He doesn't speak in the abstract; rather, he speaks in very concrete terms so the king can look at his own experience and go deeper into the true nature of things, deeper into insight.

In order to help the king realize *anicca*, the monk invites him to compare the difference in his strength at 80 to that which he had at 25.

In order to help the king realize *dukkha*, the monk invites him to consider whether there is any protection from illness.

216 • Older and Wiser

In order to help the king realize *anattā*, the monk invites him to reflect on whether or not he can take the five chords of sensual pleasure with him when he dies.

Finally, in order to help the king realize the insatiable nature of craving, the monk invites him to consider his own craving for conquest ... whether it is ever satisfied.

Do any of these four reflections speak to you more than the others? Please elaborate on how you have contemplated *anicca, dukkha, anattā* and/or the insatiable nature of craving ... and how these contemplations are helping you go beyond appearances and penetrate the deeper realities.

Reflection #3: Andrew writes, "The fourth point [the insatiable nature of craving] is probably the more illuminating one for the king to learn, because Raṭṭhapāla points out that his own desires are boundless." In a verse that concludes this particular sutta (not included here), Raṭṭhapāla recites these words: "Kings by force conquer worlds and rule the earth to the near shore but are dissatisfied and want the far shore as well. Kings and many other people go to death with craving unabated, unsated. They leave the body behind not having had enough of the world's sensual pleasures."

Can you relate to Raṭṭhapāla's teaching on the insatiable nature of craving? Have you examples of your own? Discuss this issue with your dhamma friends.

Reflection #4: In this month's sutta selection we find an interesting reversal of a common expectation. It is the young monk, not the elder king, who has the greater depth of insight. The king says that people shave their heads and go forth because of four kinds of loss – loss through aging, sickness, wealth, and relatives. He is bewildered because Raṭṭhapāla has suffered none of these and yet he has gone forth into homelessness. As elders we have the benefit of many years and much experience to help us see clearly. But deep insight can come at any time, can't it?

As an elder, have you ever noticed a tendency to talk to younger people as if they couldn't possibly understand things that you have come to know? Or, on the contrary ... have you ever found yourself listening and learning from someone much younger? What are your reflections on the timelessness of deep insight?

3.4 Getting Near the End

<u>Reflection #1</u>: How do we best prepare for our final moments? Like Ānanda, will we lose our bearings and forget everything we know? Or, like the Buddha, will we be able to transcend any pain we might feel and sustain an equanimous mental state? Obviously, we all would prefer the latter, but if we wait until our final hours to practice, it might be too late.

From time to time it can be beneficial to review the extent of our urgency in practice. Am I determined to see clearly? Am I determined to see the distinction between physical sensation and the suffering of proliferation and attachment? Am I putting my life on the line in a meaningful way? Only we know the extent of our commitment. And only we can improve our efforts.

<u>Reflection #2</u>: Andrew comments, in terms of the intense physical pain experienced by the Buddha, that it is possible to experience painful sensations as something to be investigated rather than an affliction to be resisted. This physical "sensation" is to be differentiated from the feeling tone of pleasant or unpleasant. And making the distinction between these two is one of the critical aspects of overcoming suffering.

What has been your experience in working with the sensation of intense pain? Has it been possible to investigate pain without proliferating about it, without imagining negative scenarios about its future?

<u>Reflection #3</u>: Look to the last line of the sutta: "having put away all hankering and fretting for the world." This may sound familiar to you. It appears in many suttas in the Pāli Canon (The Satipaṭṭhāna Sutta, for example) and points out that a quiet mind is both the means and the end—that is, the

218 • Older and Wiser

fertile ground that makes realization possible and the very fruit of that realization.

It seems like a powerful refrain not only in the context of Buddha's dying moment but also for living one's life. Is it possible to adopt this refrain as the key orientation for the remaining years of our life?

ILLNESS

4.1 Afflicted in Body—Not in Mind

Reflection #1: This sutta points to the need to see the difference between an afflicted body, which is inevitable, and an afflicted mind, which is optional. One who is afflicted in both body and mind does not accept the unavoidable affliction of the body and thus feels sorrow and lamentation when it occurs. One who understands that sickness and aging go with the territory of having a body lives unobsessed by false ideas and thus side-steps affliction of mind. It's pretty straight forward, isn't it? Opening to the full realization of these truths, however, may take some time.

We trace the process of our own awakening in this regard. In our youth, sickness, aging, and death may not have concerned us. But now we have the good fortune of having lived long enough to contemplate these realities through our own direct experience. We can see for ourselves how non-identification and non-attachment bring less affliction of mind.

Have you seen yourself identify with the aggregates? As you age and mature in practice, are you noticing that this tendency is diminishing? Can you offer some examples to demonstrate that through practice you are relating differently to the body? Do you find it a relief? A loss? Is there anything you'd like to say about this and about the Buddha's advice to Nakulapitā?

Reflection #2: Do you know people who, despite ample evidence to the contrary, think and behave as though they will live forever? As Andrew suggests, do you find that such denials are common? On the other hand, do you know people who, through the benefit of Buddhist teachings, are seeing in new ways, learning to relate less personally to both the body and mind? How do you relate? Share your thoughts with your dhamma friends.

Reflection #3: Gloria Taraniya refers to a common experience that she calls the pendulum swing—that is, when the body looks or feels good, we feel good; or when confronted with disagreeable mental states, we either get caught up in them or enter into battle with them? This is true of the unawakened state, isn't it? But Mu Soeng notes that while *nāma* and *rūpa* (mind and body) "cannot be made better at a biological or cellular level," we can train ourselves to accept their ups and downs as natural happenings. This is done through changes in our understanding. We see into the nature of the body and mind, and we stop being alarmed or resistant to their changing nature. Andrew states that seeing things as they actually are, rather than trying to change them or deny them, is ultimately our greatest ally as we age. What are your thoughts?

4.2   Stabbed by One Arrow—Not Two

Reflection #1: Mu Soeng points to the role that self-view plays in creating or manufacturing the second arrow. He says that the only difference between an uninstructed and an instructed person is that, while both feel the first arrow in equal measure, the uninstructed person claims ownership of the event and thus engenders an added psychological component. Another way to say this is that an uninstructed person proliferates a second arrow (a mental one) after the first one, whereas the instructed person does not.

Do you see the link between self-view, taking things personally, and the fabrication of the second arrow? You may find it helpful to discuss your experiences with your dhamma friends.

Reflection #2: Andrew writes: "Every time we have aversion toward what is unpleasant or crave for something more pleasant to arise, we are strengthening the underlying tendencies that give rise to suffering." The counterintuitive alternative is to accept things as they are. As Buddhist practitioners we discover that it isn't so easy to open in this way. Just contemplating the experience of getting older, for example, have there been times when you resisted and fought the reality of aging and what is it like to fully realize that, as Andrew writes, "resistance does not help, but only makes it hurt more"? This is the second arrow.

Reflection #3: Gloria Taraniya's reflections point to the link between opening to the first noble truth and offsetting the possibility of being stabbed by the second arrow. Have you made this kind of connection in your own practice? What are your thoughts about the importance of opening to the truth of *dukkha* as it relates to the teaching in this sutta?

Reflection #4: Whether our pain is physical or psychological, the pain is one thing, our reaction to it, another. Can you share real life situations wherein you were able to discern the difference between these two ... even while experiencing great difficulty? From your own experience, describe the impact that such a distinction is making in your life. You may prefer to describe a situation wherein you were unable to discern the difference between pain and your reaction to it.

4.3   Healing Wounds

Reflection #1: The current sutta points to the importance of tending the wound, which requires keeping it clean at all times. It calls for us to take great care, washing the wound and avoiding dust or dirt. This, says the Buddha, is necessary for healing.

Metaphorically, the Buddha is saying that the process of waking up calls for us to carefully tend and protect our insights. One is not suddenly restored with the arising of wisdom. As Andrew notes, "The behavior of the patient, as with our own conduct in the world, is an important component of deep healing." We learn to pursue only that which is suitable and avoid that which is unsuitable. Thus, craving doesn't invade the mind and we slowly stop suffering.

I suspect that you have discovered the importance of protecting your insights. How do you do this? Discuss this topic with your dhamma friends.

Reflection #2: Both Andrew and Gloria Taraniya write about the painful aspects of seeing and overcoming patterns of delusion. Andrew writes, "It hurts to see clearly, to expose the toxins at work deep in our minds. But the goal of Buddhist practice is transformation, not ease. Rooting out what causes harm, and then cutting it away once and for all with the scalpel of wisdom, is a crucial step in any program of real and lasting healing." Gloria Taraniya writes: "We seem to have to go through the painful surgical process of extracting the arrow and the surrounding poison. This is a process whereby we see for ourselves what it is like to linger in the poisonous, superficial layers of the mind where ignorance and craving dwell—ricocheting back and forth between likes and dislikes, desires and aversions, past and future."

I suspect that you know this place. How are you doing with handling it? How do you deal with the frustration and impatience that may arise in the process of purifying the mind?

Reflection #3: In her essay Gloria Taraniya writes: "As we age, quite naturally we lose interest in worldly, material things. We discover that letting go ... letting things be ... brings the greatest happiness. Sensory objects simply don't have the pull they used to have—in part because we're too tired to keep grabbing them, but also because we are garnering wisdom through years of practice."

Are you aware of increasing world-weariness that is taking place naturally as you age and as a fruit of practice? Are you finding it to be a good thing? You may find it useful to write about some of the commensurate highs and lows that you encounter or experience.

Reflection #4: This sutta talks about not incurring "death and deadly suffering." This has a technical meaning. It is death when one abandons the monastic training. It is deadly suffering when one commits an offense for which one can be expelled

222 • Older and Wiser

from the order. Although the Buddha is talking to monastics, we can find meaning here. As noted in the essay ... as lay people we do our best to "not regress on our path, revert to the old ways, or commit the kind of offenses that cause us to lose the support of our skillful companions or betray our confidence in the Buddha. Then, and only then, do we follow the true path." Any thoughts or comments?

4.4   Patient and Caregiver

Reflection #1: As Gloria Taraniya writes: "Many of the suttas in the Pāli Canon contain pithy and practical advice while fostering skillful qualities of heart." This sutta is a good example. She reminds us that how we respond in circumstances of sickness, aging, and death is predicated on our level of insight into the three characteristics of *anicca*, *dukkha* and *anatta*. Insight into *anicca* helps us be at peace in the moment because we know that conditions change; insight into *dukkha* helps us accept what might be repulsive aspects of the sick room without adding our own reactivity; insight into *anatta* helps us accept things over which we have no control.

It is important that we realize that our insights are driving our actions, even if we are not fully conscious of these. Can you think of examples wherein your insights—even if they are still not fully developed—have helped you be a better caregiver or a patient? Discuss these with your dhamma friends.

Reflection #2: Andrew notes that patient and caregiver are partners in a shared enterprise which unfolds optimally when each fulfills his or her role with integrity. It can be helpful to contemplate and discuss situations wherein you were on either side of this shared relationship. Review the qualities of both caregiver and patient outlined in this sutta and consider how you fared when you were both a caregiver or a patient. Take care to not be judgmental. The purpose of this exercise is awareness, not criticism. We want to be aware of our patterns and reactions so that we can directly determine whether or not they serve us.

Reflection #3: In addition to his essay, Mu Soeng offers a number of stories from a Korean Zen Master to help us contemplate the lessons in this sutta.

A Korean Zen master has said, "Don't wish for perfect health. In wishing for perfect health there is greed and wanting. So an ancient said, 'Make good medicine from the suffering of sickness.'" Is this saying a helpful reflection to us in crafting our own sense of an ideal patient? Does it lead further to refining our underlying sense of a reified self and how it deals with the processes of aging and sickness?

The same Korean Zen master also said: "Don't hope for a life without problems. An easy life results in a judgmental and lazy mind. So an ancient said, 'Accept the anxieties and difficulties of this life.'" Is this a helpful perspective on our practice? How big a role does "acceptance of things as they are" play in actualizing your practice? How does it help in dealing with the anxieties and difficulties that arise in connection with the processes of aging and sickness? Can our "acceptance" be proactive rather than merely passive?

The same Zen master also said: "Don't expect your practice to be always clear of obstacles. Without hindrances the mind that seeks enlightenment may be burnt out. So an ancient said, 'Attain deliverance in disturbances.'" Certainly the processes of aging, sickness, and dying bring plenty of disturbances. Does our practice enable us to rise to the challenge of dealing with these disturbances? If our practice is rooted in seeking clarity and equanimity moment after moment, should it not bring us peace in the midst of disturbances?

Death and Dying

5.1 The Divine Messengers

Reflection #1: The first lines of the poem seem to suggest that being mindful and attentive at a young age will lay down the foundations for cultivation of the noble way, for insight and understanding. As the sutta reveals, inattention can have dire consequences in this and subsequent lives. Further, the poem points to the need to contemplate our experience. Failure to do so can result in a lack of insight, and a lack of insight can result in an unhappy rebirth.

It is possible to contemplate this teaching of the divine messengers as being about actions and consequences with a certain dire outcome for misbehavior. This can be useful and can help us behave more skillfully. Wholesome habits of thought, speech, and action bring a graceful transition into mature age as well as subsequent lives, while unwholesome habits continue to produce stressful agitation and unhappy rebirth. But it is also possible to contemplate this teaching as simply a call to notice the divine messengers, contemplating their reality, and noticing our response.

How do you see the message of this sutta, and how do you work with it in your own life experience?

Reflection #2: Andrew writes that he does not take seriously the story wherein the Buddha encountered the four messengers in his youth, and that this encounter precipitated his going forth. He also does not take seriously the punishments of hell realms outlined in this story. He sees these solely as literary devices to spark our attention so that we will notice that the evidence of our mortality lies everywhere before our eyes. Whether you take these stories literally or figuratively, the point remains that it is incumbent on us to make the most of this precious human life.

What is your approach to getting the most out of life? Is that effort focused around accomplishments, checking things off your bucket list? Or is it about using your time to contemplate the nature of our existence and practicing so as to purify the heart and mind? Or both?

Reflection #3: Contemplating sickness, aging, and death can sound macabre or depressing. But as Gloria Taraniya notes there's a great paradox here. As we wake up to these seemingly grim realities, we find we are much happier because our conditioned response of longing, resistance, and ignoring diminishes. "Wow," she writes, "life includes aging, sickness, and death … and I'm okay." Seen this way, the divine messengers become the doorways to freedom and happiness.

What has been your experience in this regard? As you face and accept the realities of life and death, are you finding that you are happier? Freer? More at ease? Discuss this at length with your dhamma friends.

5.2   Learning to Let Go

Reflection #1: As we know … and may have witnessed … there are many ways to die. One might struggle and resist sickness and pain. One might bemoan pain only to see how this actually serves to increase it. As with our earlier teaching of the second arrow, this is not a helpful response. Still, it may be difficult to overcome that tendency … especially when we have spent our entire life trying to deny suffering or push it away.

Have you witnessed (or have you perhaps experienced yourself) situations that highlighted the futility of pushing pain away and, by contrast, the great value of turning towards experience and contemplating attachment and non-attachment?

Reflection #2: Perhaps the most important part of this sutta is its emphasis on the profound suffering of attachment and the great relief to be realized through non-attachment. Consider the comprehensive list of focuses for non-attachment—the six sense bases and their objects, the consciousness associated with these, the connecting link between the six senses bases and their objects, the six sense contacts, the six feelings, the four elements, the five aggregates, the four formless realms, and all that is seen, heard, thought, perceived, and investigated in the mind. It is important that we do not delay in our practice with these.

What is your experience practicing with one or another of these categories? Do you find that you are more proficient in one area than another? Write about the areas where you are most proficient and what you have learned through practicing in this way.

226 • Older and Wiser

Reflection #3: All the authors found it interesting that Venerable Sāriputta did not try to soften the blow of Anāthapiṇḍika's illness or deflect his attention by offering superficial promises of relief. Instead, he gave a teaching that implicitly acknowledged the conditions of our lives and encouraged non-attachment in relation to these.

Have you ever been in a situation—at the sickbed or deathbed of a loved one—wherein it was clear to you that the sick or dying friend or family member did not want to hear about letting go but preferred to dwell in denial? How did you handle this kind of situation? What do you think is the most-wise and compassionate response?

Reflection #4: Perhaps the greatest gift one can give a dying person would be a step-by-step invitation to release their consciousness from the attachments that constitute suffering— just as Venerable Sāriputta did with his friend Anāthapiṇḍika. What are your thoughts on this? Have you ever been called upon to do anything like this?

5.3   Taking One's Life

Reflection # 1: As Andrew notes, the Buddhist teachings seem ambiguous on the issue of suicide—seemingly stating that the integrity of one's choice or action has more to do with one's intention at the moment of the action than with the action itself. This leaves a lot of leeway for us; it is an open-hearted and non-judgmental stance. One might conclude from this analysis that when conducted with aversion or imaginings of a better life, one's intention is marred by unskillful motivations, and the outcome might be less than favorable. But it raises the question of whether or not it is possible to take one's life in a state of equanimity.

Vakkhali's story appears to address this very question. It even goes so far as to suggest that before he took his life, Vakkhali realized arahantship, thus addressing the question of whether or not an arahant can do so. This seems to say that suicide is in a different category than murder. Or does it? [In his essay, Mu Soeng alludes to other cases of monks who, though arahants themselves, committed suicide. He also offers more current-day examples that one might want to consider.]

What are your thoughts on this question of committing suicide? Can it be committed with an equanimous heart? If intention at the time of the act rules the day, can murder also be committed with an equanimous heart? Do you think it is possible?

<u>Reflection #2</u>: This sutta is appropriate even today as our culture continues to grapple with the issue of suicide—whether it is morally sound in and of itself and whether or not to legalize assisted or self-determined suicide. We all benefit from engaging in conversations on this matter. One might even say that such conversations need to happen. The Buddhist teachings offer valuable input to that conversation.

Given the complex nature of the moral and social issues and all the dilemmas that arise out of these, what criteria would you establish either from your Buddhist practice or your cultural training (or both) to determine for yourself and others whether or not you favor an absolutist position or an ambiguous one?

<u>Reflection #3</u>: This text seems to be pointing to the complex interplay of "intention" and "transgression." At what point does the wholesome clarity of intention override transgression (and any possible speculation about karmic residue)? And what does wholesome clarity of intention even mean? Perhaps, as Gloria Taraniya writes, "barring certainty that, like Vakkali, one's intention is purified of greed, hatred, and delusion … and given that, if not, the act might carry some weighty karma … perhaps the question becomes: is it worth the gamble?" In the end, it is for each of us to decide.

5.4 Facing Death Without Concern

<u>Reflection #1</u>: What do you think of the reflection from Andrew that for most people the primary concern at their deathbed is the welfare of those they are leaving behind, rather than their own pain or even the afterlife? What have you seen in the behavior of loved ones as they lay dying? Granted, unless

228 • Older and Wiser

our loved ones tell us what is in their minds our observation can only be subjective, but we can still sense where their concerns lie.

Let's take it a step further. We can say that most people find it difficult to let go if they remain concerned for the welfare of those they are leaving behind. However, turning to the needs of others may actually spring from another source. Perhaps, as Gloria Taraniya writes, such anxiety may be one of the ways that the dying person deflects his or her attention from the dying process itself—not wanting to open fully to it.

Clearly, there is a lot going on here. What are your thoughts and perspectives?

Reflection #2: Does the "stability of practice," as declared by Nakulamāta, as a result of her following the path of Dharma and Vinaya resonate for you, especially as her husband is dying? Rather than freaking out about this situation, she remains equanimous and keeps her balance.

Does this engender for you a trust in your own practice at a time of the death and sickness of those close to you or in your own sickness and dying processes?

Reflection #3: We will never know the precise moment of our own death. But we may be living our lives with the seeming conviction that death happens to other people, and will not happen to us. Does this text and the discussion around it heighten your interest in the topic in any specific way? What are its implications in your daily life?

MOURNING

6.1   Ānanda Alone

Reflection #1: In Buddhism we talk a lot about making peace with the reality of death so that when our time actually comes we are not confused or resistant. This is not to say that we cannot mourn the loss of loved ones or feel sorrow at the unavoidable prospect of our own death. Besides, opening to this reality offers great potential for liberating insight and understanding.

As a Buddhist practitioner, how have you been preparing for your own death? Beyond the worldly concerns of getting finances in order, preparing health directives, and making funeral arrangements, have you contemplated the reality of your own demise in terms of your own peace of mind? Have you moved your heart along a trajectory that promises such peace in your final moments?

Reflection #2: The message of the initial sutta in this section is quite clear. The Buddha is telling Ānanda that there is no need to resist the pain, no need to long for things to be other than they are, and that even in the face of tremendous loss, one can feel a sense of balance and well-being. As Andrew puts it: "This is liberation *within* conditions, rather than liberation *from* conditions." And as Mu Soeng puts it, this is the face of equanimity. Our task as practitioners is to "train our emotional lives to accept change and loss with a degree of equanimity. This is all the Buddha asked his followers to do."

This calls for a delicate balance between appropriate mourning and wallowing. Are you aware of the place in your own heart and in your own experience where you might cross that line between one and the other? Describe what goes on in your process of endeavoring to maintain that line.

6.2   The Mustard Seed

Reflection #1: In Gotami's story, how does the balancing of mourning for her loss and her waking up to the universal truth of grief and loss resonate for you as you walk through your own life? How does Kisa Gotami's transformation speak to you?

Reflection #2: Gloria Taraniya mentions in her comments that Kisa Gotami's story is a metaphor for progression from delusion to insight. She suggests that Gotami's story is nudging us to open our hearts so fully to the pain of the human experience that we feel

230 • Older and Wiser

the utter hopelessness of finding peace in *saṃsāra* and, thereby, turn our sights towards *nibbāna*. She asks: "How deeply must we feel the pain of delusion before we release our attachment to the world?"

Can you recall similar breakthrough moments in your awareness where insight remained stable enough for you to fundamentally change your perspectives on the nature of things?

Reflection #3: The story of Kisa Gotami is about someone waking up to the reality of impermanence and death, and then making a conscious choice to live the rest of one's days within that recognition. The Pāli term *appamāda* is sometimes translated as "care" or as someone who has come to his/her senses. The word *appamāda* is the opposite of *pamāda* which is translated as being heedless, or being drunk, out of control, or having lost one's senses. So, *appamāda* has the sense of waking up, of regaining control, of coming back to one's senses.

Kisa Gotami had a very hard lesson to learn in life. But it became a catalyst for her to regain her senses and then commit herself to the path of awakening. We all have our hard (or soft) lessons to learn in life but what's important is that we do eventually come to our senses.

What do you think?

6.3   Unbearable Grief

Reflection #1: The Buddha's advice to Patācārā to "regain her presence of mind" seems to cut to the core in terms of our own practice. As the story goes, she was mad with grief and sorrow—going over and over her sad tale—and she needed to snap out of the attachment that this necessarily involved. Once she could get outside of herself, outside of her story, she would regain her presence of mind.

Perhaps we can all relate to this aspect of the story. We know what it is like to be tormented by memories and their associated grief. But with this change in posture we can stand outside and look *at* them. What an amazing transformation this affords. This is what mindfulness makes possible.

See if you can recall a time when, like Patācārā, you found it difficult to step outside your story and/or your grief. Then recall the moment when you did. Discuss this with your dhamma friends and contemplate its significance.

Reflection #2: The Buddha advised Patācārā that there cannot be any other refuge than the clarity or presence of one's own mind. These are powerful words and, perhaps, not the kind of comforting talk we may have expected from the Buddha. But the lesson here is one that has the potential to take one all the way to freedom. His position is strong and firm and facilitates a change in Patācārā that eventually takes her all the way to freedom.

At the very least, this refusal to be overwhelmed is the Buddha's way of encouraging Patācārā to endure what needs to be endured. At best, it is a call to training in mindfulness or training in the precepts—a training that results in wisdom. Thus, all of the eightfold path is present and accounted for in the Buddha's response.

What are your thoughts on this amazing story and the Buddha's guidance to Patācārā?

Reflection #3: Patācārā's burden of grief is enormous. It's our burden too. But we each have to learn to bear that burden in our own way. How do we make our own burden light enough to bear? We cannot hide from the fact that the burdens of aging, sickness, and dying put enormous stress on our bodies and our minds. We also cannot deny our denial (light or heavy) of these burdens. We must negotiate the Middle Way here.

What useful ways have you discovered to bear this burden lightly?

232 • Older and Wiser

6.4   The Soothing of Grief

Reflection #1: There are a number of themes in this poem that are worthy of contemplation—the acknowledgement of *saṃsāra*, the endless flow of living and dying playing out within the larger journey of life, the ungraspable nature of that flow, and the uselessness of grief, a by-product of that grasping. Andrew makes a helpful observation: Patācārā's son, like all beings, was not an entity that existed as much as a unique process that occurred. "If we can not change the way things are, the skill of life becomes learning how to feel deep love and care for what is flowing through our fingers, even while letting it go." If this analysis is accurate and the Buddha's guidance here offers us the potential for liberating understanding and release, what is there left for use to do but follow suit?

How would you assess your level of understanding in this regard? Have you, as Mu Soeng notes, comprehended that "loss and death are natural recurrences in the human world"? If there is still a struggle, what are the concepts or notions or emotions that constitute that struggle? Patācārā was able to pull herself out of it. What do you think happened? What shifted for her? Can we do the same?

Reflection #2: Mu Soeng states that even in the midst of our greatest grief or greatest joy "there is a core awareness that stands outside of the experience of the moment and is able to look at it from outside." This core awareness, he says, "seems to be hardwired into our system and pops out from time to time … [It is] a neural process hardwired into our cognitive apparatus … part of the reptilian part of the brain." He notes that Patācārā was able to observe her grief through that core awareness, and that this is what helped set her free.

Each one of us has the same capacity as Patācārā. Do you have a sense of what Mu Soeng is describing here? What is your experience of it? Are you similarly able to experience the liberating aspect of such heightened awareness?

Reflection #3: In her reflection, Gloria Taraniya points to an apparent contradiction in the teachings—that is, the encouragement to open to painful feeling and embrace the realities of sickness, aging, and death on the one hand, and the importance of putting an end to grief through realizing the impermanent nature of all living things. For many people, reconciling this apparent contradiction is a process that can take many years to sort through.

You might find it helpful to read again Gloria Taraniya's thoughts on this and enter into a thoughtful discussion with your dhamma friends. To make it even more interesting, include a discussion of rebirth.

PRACTICE

7.1 The Simile of the Heartwood

Reflection #1: Is it possible to see the simile of the Heartwood as a metaphor for our own contemporary situation? Given the high standard of living that we tend to enjoy in the West, we might be inclined to hold on to material objects and comforts ... while struggling with the notion that inner renunciation is most important.

Do you agree, as the sutta suggests, that we can fall short of what we are capable of by being satisfied with superficial signs of accomplishment in our middle-class existence or the superficial levels of renunciation? In your own going forth, are you experiencing any inner tension in this regard? What are you learning?

Reflection #2: The sutta looks favorably upon the second monk as one who is not satisfied with the superficial levels of gain, honor, and renown. Instead, he makes an effort to realize "those other states that are higher and more sublime ... the unshakeable deliverance of mind."

As Gloria Taraniya notes, it behooves us to contemplate our attitudes towards both outer and inner renunciation. We can set

234 • Older and Wiser

aside material trappings, endeavor to live more simply ... and this is good. But is it enough? Are we also setting our sights on the profound letting go that characterizes inner renunciation? Can we see that this inner renunciation is none other than letting go of all levels of self-view and thereby becoming free of the anguish it causes?

Reflection #3: Some schools of thought support the idea that literal going forth into the homeless life provides the greatest support for liberation. Indeed, the Buddha himself said that going forth into monastic life is superior. Yet, he also noted that the work of liberation involves inner renunciation and transformation of an afflicted heart. What are your thoughts on the balance between inner and outer renunciation? How do they support one another? Is one more important than the other? Is psychological homelessness where the action is?

Reflection #4: In his essay Mu Soeng writes: "The last lines of this passage on the simile of the Heartwood ('This holy life does not have gain, honor, and renown as its goal. . .') is one of the most remarkable teachings in a lifetime of many remarkable teachings." If we are truly seeking to realize the ultimate level of non-attachment, it would seem that focusing on worldly gain and renown would put us at cross purposes with ourselves. What are your thoughts and reflections on this?

7.2   The Parable of Six Creatures

Reflection #1: As Gloria Taraniya notes, this sutta reminds us that in order to offset the habit of mindlessly following impulses, we need to be settled in the direct experience of the body—grounded and present. Then, like the six animals, the mind actually becomes interested in staying put. The implication here is that the mind is also "grounded in equanimity" as Andrew notes, and thus "unconcerned whether [what arises] is pleasant or unpleasant."

What is your experience of being grounded in the body? Write about what it's like to be anchored with the stake of mindfulness? Have you noticed that, when we are grounded in the body, the mind actually feels good—regardless of whether the moment is comfortable or uncomfortable?

Reflection #2: There may have been times in your life when the pull of one sense or another has gotten away from you, so to speak. Then, as Mu Soeng notes, like the six creatures " … the line between the habit force and being truly comfortable in the habitat becomes blurred." Under the impact of a perpetual sense of incompleteness, we remain confused about what we truly need or want. Contact and attachment seem to become one.

What is your experience of this? What are you learning as you practice with it?

Reflection #3: As Andrew notes, this teaching turns our notion of freedom on its head. We are used to thinking that freedom means having the ability or the freedom to follow every sensory impulse? But, as Andrew notes, the Buddha teaches us "to let go of the promise of that particular sensual gratification and return to awareness of physical sensations, even if they co-arise with feeling tones of discomfort." Thus we settle peacefully in full awareness of just what is. What are your thoughts and experiences of this profound teaching?

Reflection #4: In the first sentences of her essay, Gloria Taraniya makes the distinction between "the pull of the six senses" and "our habit of attaching to what arises at the six sense doors." This is an important distinction. We saw it in the teaching on the second arrow. We tend to feel helpless in the face of the sheer force of our habit to follow what is happening at the six sense doors. But it's our attachment that constitutes suffering, not the experience at the sense doors themselves.

Can you clearly see this distinction at moments of sensory contact? What is it like when, as Mu Soeng says, you can see the "six hungry creatures" and appreciate them without giving in to the pleasure or displeasure of consuming them"?

236 • Older and Wiser

7.3   Working with Fear

Reflection #1: Here, among other things, we see the importance of distinguishing between what is happening and our reaction to what is happening. As Mu Soeng notes, there are stories about our experiences, and there are the experiences themselves. Much of our suffering is felt when we buy in to the stories. Similarly, Taraniya notes that the highly conditioned tendency is to get lost in fear, to run away, or to ignore it—that is, to get lost in the highly conditioned responses of greed, hatred, and delusion. But this sutta demonstrates the importance of meeting things head on, standing our ground in the face of fear, keeping the mind steady and open, allowing the fear to move through.

Do you find that this is a skillful approach to freedom from fear, especially as it relates to fear of sickness, aging, and death? Please elaborate on your response.

Reflection #2: Among other things, this sutta points to the correlation between ethical conduct and the absence of fear. In other suttas the Buddha states that by keeping the precepts we give each other the gift of fearlessness. Perhaps, as Andrew notes, when we misbehave we suffer from guilt and shame, which are the true sources of our fear.

What is your experience of this? Do you see a correlation between ethical conduct and the presence or absence of fear? How do you work with anxiety regarding past unskillful actions?

Reflection #3: Mu Soeng notes that liberation involves confronting both psychological fear and the primal fear of extinction ... and that the latter is more primary. The Buddha seems to be saying that setting up practices or situations to dampen or diminish such highly conditioned patterns of fear and dread can be a very skillful undertaking. In fact, he consciously confronted these primal fears of biological extinction by putting himself in dangerous situations in the forest.

I'll bet you have practice stories wherein you have done just this ... made strong determinations *(adhiṭṭhānas)* to see your fear through. Contemplate your experiences. What are you learning as you practice with fear?

7.4 Living in Harmony

Reflection #1: Are you aware of the relentless habit of the mind to find fault with self and others, to set up battle stations, and/or proliferate about seemingly everything? Have you ever felt frustrated at not being able to stop getting caught up in a quarrelsome mind? As mature practitioners, we are all trying new things, endeavoring to understand what the mind is doing and to stop being caught up in difficult or useless states of mind. What are your thoughts on all of this?

Reflection #2: The sutta asks us to consider what is more important—being right and winning arguments or living together in harmony? While, as Andrew notes, there may be some situations in which a great deal is at stake, "most of our quarrels fall well below this threshold, and most of the wounds we inflict with our words are not warranted." Through practice ... and as we get older ... many practitioners state feel naturally more inclined to remain open-minded when facing conflicting perspectives, to simply notice those moments when we disagree, accept these as standard operating procedure, and to let imperfect moments arise and pass away without quarrels or even comments.

Has this been your experience? Do you have some experiences you would like to share? Is it different when a great deal is at stake? What do you do then?

Reflection #3: The sutta mentions six principles that are conducive to living together in harmony—kindness in body, speech, and mind, sharing, virtuous conduct, and right view.

Please discuss the importance of any of the six principles included in this text ... or simply write about an example of any one of these. Do you agree with Gloria Taraniya's comment that right view may be the most important?

GOING FORTH: From Home to Homelessness
Essay by Mu Soeng

"Going Forth" (Pāli: *pabbajana*; Skt: *pravraajana*) is a term of great antiquity in broader Indian philosophical thought, and seems to have been a core reference point for religious rebels at the time of the Buddha. It refers to a clarion call for "going forth from home life to homelessness" that was quite audible and visible at the time of Buddha's birth. It was seen in the figure of the wandering ascetic whose sighting became one of the four "heavenly signs" the young and safely-ensconced Siddhartha Gautama saw: an old man, a sick person, a corpse, and the wandering ascetic. These four signs were disturbing enough for the young man to go forth from his comfortable life of luxury and security to live as an ascetic in the forest. Until very recently, the figure of an ochre-robed *sannyasin*, the wandering ascetic, was so common in the cities and towns of India as to be part of the scenery that everyone took for granted.

The protocols of Going Forth at the time of the birth of the Buddha effectively meant leaving the life of a civic society and becoming a wandering ascetic, often joining a group of ascetics. The central fact of the future Buddha going into the forest remained the physical act of leaving a domestic life. Within the Buddhist tradition this call got translated, centuries after the death of the Buddha, into settled monasticism. The physical act of joining a community of monks has remained the most visible dimension of Going Forth in the life of a Buddhist.

In recent years, Sangharakshita, the British-born former Buddhist monk and founder of Western Buddhist Fellowship, has broadened the definition of "Going Forth" in interesting ways that go beyond the conventional monastic context:

> *[Sangharakshita] understands Going Forth as the act of taking personal responsibility for oneself and one's development independent of*

the views and conventions of the society in which one belongs. In his terminology Going Forth is the act whereby the individual separates himself from the 'group'—the group being the various overlapping collectivities to which human beings belong and which are organized for their survival, exacting subservience to norms and customs as the price of protection and aid. Going Forth from the group is therefore a key step in spiritual life, since it is only as an individual that one can develop on the path. Going Forth does not, however, mean hostility to the group—merely that one is not, or is less and less, bound by its norms and customs. ("Going Forth and Citizenship" by Subuthi, Western Buddhist Fellowship website).

The Historical Background

In trying to understand the contexts in which the norms of Going Forth among the wandering ascetics were contesting the established order of things in ancient India, the following observation from Sukumar Dutt's classic study of the protocols of early Buddhist monks (*Buddhist Monks and Monasteries of India*) seems to be quite helpful:

To the makers of the Dharmasastras [the literature of the Vedic Aryan civilization] the Vedic Aryan tradition contemplates only the householder's life: it sanctions and supports only this ashrama. The Parivrajaka, the wandering almsman, is a recusant from it in his going 'from home into homelessness', a custom bereft of Vedic sanction … 'the way of Brahma-seeking', it is said, is not for householders, but only for the homeless. The standpoint of those who give the call to a higher-than-social life is necessarily different from those to whom the stability of society is the be-all and end-all…. Some of the latter-day authors of Dharamsastras assail the Upanisadic ashrama theory of 'life in stages' on the ground that it is not 'seen' in the Vedas in which only one stage, viz., that of the householder is contemplated.

The ashrama theory referred to in the above passage speaks of four stages of life for a noble (Aryan) person: 1) *Brahmacharya* —the life of a celibate student working in close contact with a teacher; 2) *Grahasta*—the life of a married householder; 3) *Vanaprastha*—the stage where both husband and wife leave home after their children have grown up and have children of their own, to join a community of "retired" folks in the forest; and 4) *Sannyasin*—the stage where husband and wife separately leave the community upon intimation of infirmity and/or approaching death, and wander around in the forest until the moment of death.

It should be noted that a) this system emerged as a result of various accommodations and arrangements between the older Vedic culture and the highly visible culture of wandering ascetics in pre-Buddhist India; and b) it was put into practice by a relatively small number of people who had internalized the classical teachings on life and death. It was not for the faint of the heart. Nonetheless, as a cultural norm, it remains the defining feature of an evolved religious life in all Indian traditions, including Hinduism, Buddhism, Jainism, and others.

The classical Vedic culture (circa 1500-800 BCE) was centered on sacrifice (animals and grain) as ritual action (karma), which sustained the human afterlife, the gods, and the cosmos. The Indus Valley culture preceding it (circa 2500-1500 BCE) seems to have been organized around Fertility Goddess cults and/or symbolism associated with yogic practices. In the ascendant Vedic society, the esoteric knowledge of the Vedic priest (the Brahmin), in conducting the sacred ritual and his correct intonation of sacred *mantras*, was seen as key to controlling the external world. It was also seen as a method for generating inner heat that epitomized the magical efficacy of the rituals performed externally. It was a system of "acquisition of power," and we can see its historical evolution along these lines:

1) Yogic culture of Indus Valley civilization offering possibility of magical or political power through yogic practices;

2) Early Vedic culture of Northwestern India creating a culture of ritual sacrifice around a circle of fire (*dhuni*) as a tool for calling upon gods and getting their protection in various enterprises on earth; a system of acquiring magical and political power;

3) Later Vedic culture internalizing sacrificial symbolism and moving from priestly ritual to yogic practices largely under the influence of wandering ascetics who might have been remnants of older Indus Valley culture, and who had regrouped themselves as followers of Jain tradition in pre-Buddhist India;

4) Post-Vedic culture of the Upanishads creating a new definition of karma through intentional action rather than its being generated in ritual action/sacrifice. This definition created a new relationship between the human being and the cosmos in which knowledge of the Absolute (Brahman) and the ontological status of the Self (atman) becomes pivotal.

The eastward expansion of the geographical frontier of Aryan civilization and its role in facilitating the emergence of *paribajjika* (wandering ascetics) is a little known but instructive chapter in that story. This expansion may have started some two to three hundred years before the birth of the Buddha, and it is not unlike the Westward push of the American frontier before and after the Civil War, which allowed for a new vision of the individual and society to emerge in contrast to how the Puritans of New England had defined them up to that time.

Thus, it would seem that the institution of the *sannyasin*, the ubiquitous figure of a wandering renunciate in Hindu India, is a much later development, and seemingly greatly impacted by the wandering ascetics of the shramana tradition that was developed and honed in the new geographical areas of Magadha, the kingdom in eastern India that became home to a large population of ascetics. Rajagaha (Skt: Rajagraha), the ancient capital of this kingdom, was home to three highly-prominent religious personalities of sixth century BCE: the Buddha; Mahavira, the last great figure of Jain religion; and Makkali Gosala, the putative founder of Ajivika sect. There were doubtless many other ascetic sects that are now lost to history.

What follows from this is that the four-fold stages of life (ashrama) theory in the literature of later Hindu generations really emerged out of the powerful *leitmotif* of renunciation in shramana culture. Thus it is the ascetics of Buddhist, Jain, and other traditions who basically transformed Indian religious culture in lasting ways, making renunciation such an important part of Hindu religious thought that it came to be integrally identified with it. The fact that the *sannyasin*, the renunciate, is now such a defining feature of Hindu religious thought is a remarkable turnaround from the original model in the Vedas of a householder's life.

A New Interpretation

In my own reflections on how the term Going Forth can conceivably speak to us within the contexts of our own twenty-first century sensibilities and realities, I have come to see it as "going forth into psychological homelessness" rather than the conventional physical homelessness. It seems to me that an emphasis on psychological homelessness and a consequent de-emphasis on physical homelessness offers a much more nuanced correlate to the exhortation of the Buddha to his followers: live a life of non-clinging. What is important to note about Buddha's teachings is that a life of non-clinging is not *ultimately* dependent on physical homelessness; it can be achieved as well, perhaps more so, through psychological homelessness.

What can possibly explain the roots of psychological homelessness or non-clinging? The broadest understanding we have from our discussion about the culture of wandering ascetics in India is that it is rooted in recognizing the futility of worldly pleasures as a source of true happiness. The ubiquitous word in Indian philosophical and religious traditions really speaks to this sense of futility: *saṃsāra*. In a simple translation, *saṃsāra* means the phenomenal world: the world of senses and sense-pleasures. For the Buddha, the phenomenal world was a place of craving and clinging (for the ignorant person) and therefore a source of suffering. A wise person can train himself or herself to negotiate the pitfalls of the phenomenal world without craving and clinging. That would be the end of suffering for the wise person.

A proper understanding of Buddha's emphasis on craving and clinging does not make it "pessimistic" or "world-denying" as has often been claimed by its opponents. For Buddhists, it is simply a quantifiable and a demonstrative equation: if you cling to the phenomenal world, you will suffer; if you do not cling, you will be free from suffering.

What then is *saṃsāra?* The Buddha spoke often of the three poisons of greed, hatred, and delusion. But in the broader Indian tradition, there is a step further back that speaks of the so-called five poisons of food, sleep, sex, fame, and wealth as the loci of greed, hatred, and delusion. No doubt the powerful drives of greed, hatred, and delusion work separately and collectively in tandem with each of the five poisons.

The presence of these five poisons and our craving and clinging for them is not a metaphysical issue; these are hard, existential presences in the lives of each one of us. As our conditioned existence becomes more negatively complex, each of these poisons coalesce around metaphysical and conceptual constructs such as self, afterlife, past, future, good, bad, and so on.

In the Indian and Buddhist traditions, *saṃsāra* and *dukkha* are almost synonymous terms. It was not only the Buddha who emphasized the centrality of *dukkha* in human condition, but also the broader Indian philosophical tradition, which has been in agreement in recognizing the transience and dissatisfactory nature of human existence. It is only in formulating an escape or transcendence from *dukkha* that the Buddha and other Indian thinkers differ from one another. It is not surprising then that they all found a common ground in Going Forth: a householder's life is dusty and not conducive to a higher calling. One does one's duty (dharma) by one's family, but one is always aware of Plan B (husband and wife leaving home to enter a forest community) and Plan C (husband and wife separately leaving that community upon intimation of infirmity and death and wandering around as *sannyasin*). In other words, an overarching intention or sensibility has been put into each individual's psyche from very early on that determines how and in what ways he or she will engage with the phenomenal world.

The logic of this orientation of being in the world suggests that one cultivates a dispassionate approach to engagement with worldly affairs. One does what needs to be done but also recognizes that these worldly engagements are a hindrance to the ultimate goal of liberation (Skt: *moksha*; in Hindu tradition). In this orientation, leaving home to join a forest community in one's middle age is not an afterthought arising out of some existential crisis or trauma, but an organic unfolding of how one has always been in the world.

This dispassion toward worldly affairs is a core ingredient for psychological homelessness. Understood properly, it is not simply an individual issue but a collective one as well. If the value system of an entire society is not geared for striving for worldly success, what does it say about the notions of "progress," "improvement," or "success"? These differences in the so-called Eastern and Western ways of thinking are now front and center in public discourse around issues of what it means to be in the world and what it means to live a "meaningful life."

Psychological Homelessness

Our challenge then is to understand what this dispassion, this psychological homelessness, means for living a Buddhist life. Traditionally it means an end to suffering through attaining *nirvāna*. But here we run into doctrinal difficulties of trying to explicate what *nirvāna* means. For many people *nirvāna* is a mystical experience that transcends human experience. Even among Buddhist teachers, there is no consensus in interpreting *nirvāna*.

But it may be possible to suggest that the *nirvāna* (or any mystical) experience does induce a sense of dispassion in the subject. We can perhaps go one more step and suggest that a common theme that can be identified in all these mystical experiences, though not always talked about, is a sense of a phenomenal world that is stifling in its multiplicity. In other words, the more complex the multiplicity, the more stress is felt in the awareness matrices of the experiencing subject. This stress is quantifiable as the inability of awareness to process all the data coming into the perceptual-cognitive field. In "Strangers to Ourselves: Discovering the Adaptive Unconscious," the cognitive scientist Timothy Wilson writes that in each second we have nearly two million bits of data coming in, but our conscious mind can process only forty of them. Our mind's inability to process all that it is coming into contact with becomes a source of stress and anxiety in an untrained mind.

The subjective experience of a meditative state, on the other hand, shows that it is possible to let go of multiplicity while focusing instead on a chosen object of awareness, such as the breath coming in and going out. In this meditative state, there is a quantifiable lessening of stress. In other words, with training one lets go of the "filters" that have been put into place in our normal conditioning to obscure the child-like innocence and curiosity that is still there in the background as our evolutionary inheritance. Letting go of these filters is a recovery of that child-like state, at least for a short period of time, leaving one feeling refreshed and recharged. We need not enter into obscure philosophical arguments about whether to call such an experience "unitary consciousness" or some other positivistic designation. It can be said with some degree of confidence, however, that the experience of letting go of the accumulated filters in our awareness is accessible to anyone with some training in discipline.

This discussion is relevant only to the extent that in our normal human conditioning we find a "home" in the filters: the "poisons" of food, sex, sleep, fame, wealth, and a vast array of subsets of them. Our craving and clinging in varying degrees to each becomes a kind of virus that infects the total environment and entrenches itself through normative drives of greed, hatred, and delusion.

There seems to have been a spoken and unspoken recognition among Buddhist and Hindu householders in Asian history that finding a "home" in *saṃsāra* and its consequent "poisons" is a recipe for putting oneself in bondage in all the birth cycles. There is a corresponding recognition of the limitations and futility of these poisons in providing lasting happiness, as well as a sense of "shame" in aligning one's efforts in pursuing one or many of them. It is this sense of shame that gives urgency to embracing the stage of life where one is able to leave home and hearth and be in an environment where one does not have to be in bondage to these poisons.

So we come to the proposition that "leaving home" and "going forth into homelessness" is not so much about a physical structure of a home but the "home" we have created for the pursuit of the five poisons as the operating principles of our life. Correspondingly, "homelessness" is not so much about being in the forest (although that does help) but disenchantment with, dispassion for, and non-pursuit of the temptations and seductions of the poisons.

Whether one leaves the physicality of a home is largely a matter of detail, at least in my understanding. I like to think that it is possible for a trained person to live the life of an urban hermit in New York City with just as much discipline as a monk lives in the forest. The urban hermit can create a daily structure in much the same way that a forest hermit does; he or she can step outside the apartment with as much dispassion, detachment, and equanimity as does a forest hermit.

Human experience shows that connecting with psychological homelessness in a positive way is a powerful incentive, especially in middle-age years, to uncover the layers of disenchantment, alienation, stress, and unsatisfactoriness that have been there all along as part of our life experience, which we have continued to either suppress or deny. Buddha's teachings see going forth into psychological homelessness as a creative act of re-evaluation of our human life. It is the beginning of a new chapter in our human journey where we relearn to view the world with fresh new eyes.

Urban Hermit: A Different Way of Being in the World
Essay by Mu Soeng

In the fall of 2013, I was fortunate enough to undertake a three-month meditation/writing retreat in a small cabin in Vermont. The cabin belongs to a friend who lives in a similar cabin next door. As it turned out, being in proximity to this friend (who I shall call Walter) and getting to know him a little better was perhaps the most rewarding part of my retreat.

Walter was inspired to experiment with how a modern-day Thoreau would create his own Walden Pond. He had enough savings to have a simple cabin built for himself that was aesthetically pleasing but wrapped in utter simplicity. The cabin has a loft but no bedroom—just a mattress that he unrolls at night.

Walter does not have a car or a computer or a television. No smartphone either, but plenty of shelves groaning with books. The only somewhat modern technology in his cottage is a land-line telephone, gas stove, and water heater. He has a typewriter on which he does his writing and a bicycle that he uses to visit friends and shop for groceries.

With an inspired sense of generosity, Walter had another cabin built next to his own. He set up a program to allow artists and writers to come and spend a few days to work on their projects in this second cabin. He doesn't accept any money for such stays and encourages those using the cabin to donate to a charity of their choice. He was kind enough to let me use the cabin for such a long period of time.

I later found out that the local paper had done a profile on Walter in which it was asserted that he probably had the smallest carbon footprint of anyone in the entire state. The same profile also mentioned that in his will he had donated his two cabins to the local arts council so that artists could continue to use these places to do their work in seclusion.

Walter's daily routine begins around 5am with sitting in silent vigil/prayer (he affiliates himself with the Unitarian Church), after which he has a simple breakfast of granola. The rest of his morning he spends quietly reading and writing. He skips lunch because, as he says, he "doesn't need it." His dinner consists of simple brown rice, tofu, and vegetables from the garden behind his cabin. His evenings are spent in quiet contemplation, and he goes to bed shortly after dark.

When I asked Walter if he considered himself a hermit, he said he preferred the word *solitary* because he was trying to engage with others in a more skillful way, not cut himself off from the world. He also attends the weekly meetings of the local Unitarian Church and helps out at a local food co-op.

Walter is in his early seventies and quite fit and healthy for his age. He had already been carving out his solitary existence for about twenty years when I got to know him. By my reckoning, he has succeeded in becoming a modern-day Thoreau.

Since I was working on a writing project on Buddha's teachings on the training of a noble person, Walter's embodiment of an urban hermit was much more resonant for me than I could have expected when I first made plans to go stay in the cabin. The biggest overlap between what Walter was doing and what was being proposed in Buddha's teaching was the separation of needs from wants.

William Powers, a senior fellow at the World Policy Institute, has recently taken on a leadership role in the global "Slow Movement." As part of his own personal involvement in slowing down, he spent a season in a 12-foot-by-12-foot cabin off the grid in North Carolina. He wrote about his experiment in an award-winning memoir called *Twelve by Twelve: A One-Room Cabin Off the Grid and Beyond the American Dream* (2010). His follow-up experiment of living in a tiny apartment in Manhattan was motivated to a large extent by a somewhat angry question from a reader of the book. "It's easy," she had written, "to find minimalism, joy, connection to nature, and abundant time in a shack in the woods. But how the hell are the rest of us supposed to stay sane in our busy modern lives?"

So, Powers and his wife jettisoned 80 percent of their belongings and moved from their 2,000-square-foot townhouse in Queens, across the river to a 350-square-foot micro-apartment in Greenwich Village. Their attempt to live slowly and mindfully in frantic Manhattan is recounted in *New Slow City: Living Simply in the World's Fastest City* (2014).

In many ways, the experiment conducted by the Powers in New York City provides a bookend to how Walter in Vermont has been experimenting with his own life. Both were seeking an answer to the same question: Is it actually possible to leave only the tiniest carbon footprint regardless of where you happen to be living? While Walter was inspired by Henry David Thoreau, Powers has spent two decades exploring the speed of American culture and its alternatives in some fifty countries around the world. He has been a leader in development and conservation movements in Latin America, Africa, and North America. But what makes Powers different from other writers on conservation and/or mindfulness is that he and his wife actually put their lives on the line.

Many years ago, I came to know two Westerners in their late thirties or early forties who had become students of a Tibetan lama. They and other like-minded people had pooled their resources to rent a big house in Toronto where they and their teacher could all live and practice. These two—a man and a woman, though not a couple—worked at the large postal sorting facility where I also worked for one summer.

They had chosen to work at the post office because sorting an unending mountain of mail was in many ways an ideal activity for continuing and deepening their meditation practice. Their value system was centered around ethical living in their small community of Buddhist practitioners—a simple life without television or any overt forms of entertainment.

252 • Older and Wiser

These three narratives all have their own trajectories and unique worldviews and intentions, but together they create a space for the beginning of a conversation about the paradigm of an urban hermit. In many ways, such a conversation has been and continues to be taboo among philosophers and culture-shapers.

An urban hermit is not an identity but a felt-sense of being in the world. A "felt-sense" is by definition both fluid and guided by one or more specific principles or questions. A case can be made that we all have a felt-sense of struggling to be at peace within ourselves regardless of the many ways in which our conditions and circumstances may differ. For many, the idea of solitude, of being alone for a short or long period of time, may be an appealing way to disengage from pressures that create and define the struggle to be at peace with ourselves in the first place.

The three narratives above all seem to have been informed by a desire, a need perhaps, for solitude. All of these people were aware, at some level, of the need to create some distance between their inner lives and the fragmentation produced by a chaotic social setting and work culture in a post-industrial society, particularly its American version in the late twentieth and early twenty-first centuries.

Jiddhu Krishnamurti, the famous Indian philosopher, has said,

> *To be alone is essential for man to be uninfluenced, for something uncontaminated to take place. For this aloneness there seems to be no time. There are too many things to do, too many responsibilities and so on. To learn to be quiet, shutting oneself in one's room, to give the mind a rest, becomes a necessity. Love is part of this aloneness. To be simple, clear, and inwardly quiet is to have that flame. Things may not be easy, but the more one asks of life, the more fearful and painful it becomes. To live simply, uninfluenced, though everything and everyone is trying to influence, to be without varying moods and demands, is not easy, but without a deep, quiet life, all things are futile.* ("Letters to a Young Friend," 20)

Ivan Illich (1926-2002) was as an urban hermit of an altogether different type. He lived his life as a homeless intellectual and worked tirelessly to make the world a better place. Illich was born in Vienna to a Croatian Catholic engineer father and a Sephardic Jewish mother. He grew up speaking Italian, Spanish, French, and German. He later learned Croatian, ancient Greek, Latin, Portuguese, Hindi, and English. A brilliant scholar, he studied histology and crystallography at the University of Florence in Italy, and then theology and philosophy at the Pontifical Gregorian University at the Vatican.

Despite his heavily-educated background, Illich became a highly-influential critic of institutionalized education. In his book *Deschooling Society* he advocated a system of self-directed education, opposing what he felt were deadening institutional restrictions. He also became a critic of international aid programs, which he saw largely as attempts to impose Western industrial hegemony on the developing world.

In 1951, he became a parish priest in Washington Heights, one of New York City's poorest neighborhoods, then a barrio of freshly-arrived immigrants from Puerto Rico. In 1956, at the age of 30, he was appointed vice-rector of the Catholic University of Puerto Rico but was thrown out a few years later because of his loud criticism of Vatican positions on birth control and nuclear weapons.

In 1959, Illich traveled throughout South America on foot and by bus. In 1961, he founded the Centro Intercultural de Documentación (CIDOC or Intercultural Documentation Center), which became part language school and part free university for intellectuals and hippies from all over the Americas. Illich remained a Roman Catholic priest his entire life, continually criticizing the institutions of Western culture (including the Vatican) and their effects on education, medicine, work, energy use, transportation, and economic development.

Illich did not choose to spend his life in cloistered monasteries. His intellectual and vocational engagements were always in the midst of high-intensity urban areas. In the 1970s and 1980s, he became friends with Jerry Brown, the once and

254 • Older and Wiser

future governor of California, who described Illich's life in these words:

> *[Illich] had no home of his own and relied on the hospitality of friends. He traveled from place to place with never more than two bags. He refused medical diagnosis, any form of insurance, and gave away whatever savings remained at the end of each year.*
>
> *Among the serious thinkers I have had the privilege to meet, Ivan Illich alone embodied in his personal life as well as in his work a radical distancing from the imperatives of modern society.*
>
> *Ivan Illich was the rarest of human beings: erudite, yet possessed of aliveness and sensitivity. He savored the ordinary pleasures of life even as he cheerfully embraced its inevitable suffering. Steeped in an authentic Catholic tradition, he observed with detachment and as a pilgrim the unforgiving allure of science and progress. With acute clarity and sense of humor, he undermined, in all that he wrote, the uncontested certitudes of modern society.*
>
> *In the last twenty years of his life, Ivan Illich suffered increasingly from a persistent growth on the side of his face, which he never treated, nor had diagnosed. In explaining why he voluntarily suffered, he said simply: "Nudum Christum nudum sequere." I follow the naked Christ.*
>
> *In what was his most provocative and perhaps final comment on the pursuit of health, Illich wrote: "Yes, we suffer pain, we become ill, we die. But we also hope, laugh, celebrate; we know the joy of caring for one another; often we are healed and we recover by many means. We do not have to pursue the flattening-out of human experience. I invite all to shift their gaze, their thoughts, from worrying about health care to cultivating the art of living. And, today with equal importance, the art of suffering, the art of dying.* (Whole Earth Catalog, Spring 2003)

An urban hermit is inspired to turn inevitabilities into art forms—the art of living, the art of being alone, the art of serving others, the art of dying—and to train himself or herself in orienting to life as an opportunity for learning, exploring, and seeing what is and what is not possible. One finds a principle or a question, an image or a feeling, and one follows it—wherever it might lead, however long it feels worth following.

Most of us have imagined what it would be like to live in a completely different way. We all seem to believe there's something in particular waiting to be discovered in a deeper inner or outer solitude—the promise that there just might be a radically different way to depend on and relate to the world and one another.

Illich's vision of the self in society mirrors what Martin Luther King once said during his "Beyond Vietnam" address at a New York City church in 1967: "We must rapidly begin the shift from a thing-oriented society to a person-oriented society. When machines and computers, profit motives and property rights, are considered more important than people, the giant triplets of racism, materialism, and militarism are incapable of being conquered."

While Illich and King emphasized the participatory activity of self in society, Walter and Powers have leaned toward solitude and inward contemplation. The model of the urban hermit is a spectrum, not a fixed point. All who are so drawn will sketch out different maps and be guided by variously-constructed compasses. Regardless of the countless ways one may travel from point A to point B a single question is likely to guide and support all paths: What kind of sensitivity can I bring to the many pushes and pulls of greed, hatred, and delusion?

About the Authors

Mu Soeng is the study center's program director and resident scholar. He trained in the (Korean) Zen tradition and was a monk for eleven years. He is the author of *Thousand Peaks: Korean Zen (Tradition and Teachers); The Diamond Sutra: Transforming the Way We Perceive the World; Trust in Mind: The Rebellion of Chinese Zen;* and *The Heart of the Universe: Exploring the Heart Sutra.*

Gloria Taraniya Ambrosia teaches within the Thai Forest Tradition, specifically the disciples of Ajahn Chah. She is a Lay Buddhist Minister in association with Abhayagiri Buddhist Monastery in California. Taraniya served as resident teacher of the Insight Meditation Society in Barre, Massachusetts from 1996 through 1999. She currently teaches at the IMS Forest Refuge and is a core faculty member at the Barre Center for Buddhist Studies. She has been a Dhamma teacher since 1990.

Andrew Olendzki was trained in Buddhist Studies at Lancaster University in England, as well as at Harvard and the University of Sri Lanka. Formerly executive director of IMS, executive director of BCBS, and editor of the *Insight Journal,* he is the author of *Unlimiting Mind* and *Untangling Self*

Barre Center for Buddhist Studies

The Barre Center for Buddhist Studies is a non-profit educational organization dedicated to exploring Buddhist thought and practice as a living tradition, faithful to its origins, yet adaptable to the current world. The Center, located in Barre, Massachusetts, offers residential and online courses combining study, discussion, and meditation for the purpose of deepening personal practice while building and supporting communities of like-minded practitioners. Our programming is rooted in the classical Buddhist tradition of the earliest teachings and practices, but calls for dialogue with other schools of Buddhism and with other academic fields—and with each other. All courses support both silent meditation practice and critical, dialogical investigation of the teachings.

BCBS was founded in 1991 by teachers at Insight Meditation Society (IMS), including Joseph Goldstein and Sharon Salzberg, and is connected to both IMS and the Forest Refuge by trails through the woods.

BCBS is committed to cultivating a community that reflects the diversity of our society and our world. We seek to promote the inclusion, equity and participation of people of diverse identities so that all may feel welcome, safe, and respected within this community. Find out more about our mission, our programs, and sign up for our free monthly e-newsletter at www.bcbsdharma.org

Printed in Great Britain
by Amazon